**Communication and Information Research Group Number 3**

# 'A Communication Studies Approach to Children's Literature'

David Rudd

## Acknowledgements

This work is adapted from my M.A. Communication Studies dissertation. I am thus indebted to the staff of the Department of Communication Studies, and especially to my supervisors, Ros Brunt and Martin Jordin. Also, my thanks to the teachers and pupils at 'Cloverdale', 'Clogburn' and 'Sprawldon' schools - who must regrettably remain anonymous (but an especial thank you to Penney, Albert and Chloe). Thanks too, to the Bolton Schools Library Service for their bibliographical expertise, to my work colleagues, and, more personally, to Rae and Sue, for putting me up/up with me in Sheffield. Lastly,thanks to Sheena, Duncan and Sophie, for giving me space, support and endless cups of coffee.

0863393195

# Contents

3703821128

A
PAVIC
PUBLICATION
from Library & Learning Resources

© 1992 ISBN 0 86339 3195

"...what is the use of a book ....without pictures or conversations?"

(Lewis Carroll)

**Abstract**

This work explores three related issues: (1) that children's literature is generally appropriated by adults, marginalising children's own views; (2) even thus appropriated, children's literature remains a peripheral concern of those disciplines that do deal with it - chiefly Literary Studies and Education/developmental psychology; (3) that a Communication Studies approach, using a Foucauldian notion of 'discourse', offers a fresh approach: not only does it seek to explain the reasons for (1) and (2), but it also establishes, as a methodological principle, that any study of children's literature should place it in a concrete social context, thus giving more space to children's own views.

Both literary and psychological studies are re-examined in the light of this approach. Roald Dahl's **The Twits** is then taken as an example of a text liked by children, albeit the butt of much adverse adult criticism. The various discursive threads of the story are examined before groups of children drawn from three different schools are questioned about their appreciation of it. As a result, it is suggested that a Communication Studies approach is fruitful and worthy of further investigation for several reasons: firstly it offers a broad-based, interdisciplinary approach united around the concept of 'discourse'; secondly, it is always sensitive to the socio-historical context; thirdly, it sees children's literature in the context of other areas of social life (i.e. of signification), rather than as an exclusive realm; fourthly, it recognises the unequal power relationships that constitute its status; finally, it seeks to explore children's literature in concrete social contexts, to prevent the current endless, abstract appropriations.

---

Unlike the terms 'children's art', or 'children's writing', 'children's literature' expresses a lack of ownership: it is literature **for**, not **of** the child; it is written, vetted, published, disseminated and evaluated by others. To some extent, this has to be so - but not to the extent that generally prevails, as the exceptions make plain. Children have shown themselves capable of writing, reviewing and undertaking surveys (e.g. Doherty, 1987, 1989; Fillingham, 1989).

However, children's strongest claims to ownership of their literature are expressed in the way they appropriate or reject specific works. It is interesting to note the differences here between expert lists (e.g. Butler, 1986; Hollindale, 1974) and surveys of children's own preferences (Crowther, 1986; Ingham, 1981; Westall, 1985; Whitehead, et al., 1977). Most recently the contrast was brought home in Hill (1989), where adult experts and children each selected fifty favourite titles, only a few of which overlapped.

In this work I want to probe the way children are marginalised in considerations of their literature. But there seems to be more to it than just ignoring the child, for children's literature is itself generally ignored, both in the book world and by academia. Thus, despite being a major area of publishing both in the nineteenth century and now, children's

**Chapter 1 - Introduction**

5

literature seems to be regarded as inferior. Although its market share doubled between 1981 and 1989, its authors and editors are paid less, its advertising budgets are minimal, and 95% of its books are not reviewed (Nettell, 1990). It is also worth noting that not only is it associated with children, but also particularly with women, both as writers, and as buyers (63% are women - anon, 1991).

Turning to the academic world, the story is similar. Despite cries like Shavit's (1986, p. x) - 'I believe the time has come to extricate children's literature from the narrow boundaries of the past and to place it in the foreground of literary scholarship' - the establishment is generally unimpressed. A recent reference book on literature (Coyle et al., 1990), though it aims to be comprehensive, discussing all types of genre, women's literature, 'new' literatures - even 'folk literature' - still ignores children's literature throughout its 1,299 pages. This absence is also reflected in higher education literature courses, though other less traditional forms (e.g. women's writing, sf, romance) are increasingly featured. For the study of children's literature, one must look to teaching and librarianship courses - to professions, it should be noted, strongly associated with women.

In my research, therefore, I shall also be investigating the positioning of children's literature in the academic discourses of literature and education/developmental psychology. However, there is a third area of neglect. For Communication Studies also seems to have little to say about the topic. Workers in this area tend to couple children with television (e.g. Eagleton, 1983, p.

211), just as women are frequently associated with romance, and youth with music. Thus a third aim of this work is to suggest how a Communication Studies approach might be fruitful, both in explaining the adult appropriation, and in showing a way in which children's own meanings can be given more space (1).

First, though, it is important to define these terms. By a 'Communication Studies' approach I mean one which gives more emphasis to how meanings are constructed, circulated, and appropriated by different groups in different social contexts, and especially as to why some meanings have more currency than others. The term 'discourse' seems particularly useful here, in that it is one of the few concepts used across the various disciplines, albeit in rather different and sometimes nebulous ways. For this reason, I shall now spend some time clarifying my usage of the term 'discourse', both as a theoretical concept, and as a methodological principle.

The term discourse is often used to name units of text larger than the sentence (e.g. Brown & Yule, 1983; Stubbs, 1983). Whilst this is a useful label, I would like to give it a twist (following Foucault and others) and suggest that discourses are themselves what texts are constructed from. A text, in other words, has 'texture': it is a weave of different voices (Barthes, 1975). Identifying these discourses is difficult however, for two interrelated reasons: firstly, because we are implicated in their construction; indeed, it is only because we can trade on this process that we recognise them at all. This means, secondly, that discourses never stand still; they are always 'under construction'. In other words, they are practices, rather than objects with particular linguistic features.

There are two common reactions to this, from which I should like to distance myself. I shall call them 'subjectivism' and 'determinism' respectively. The subjectivist view, common to much post-structuralist interpretation, is to see the constructive process as one of freewheeling individual creativity. This is mistaken, in that the discourses we use always precede us, informing what we say, how we say it, and how it is likely to be interpreted. Discourses always have historical precedents sedimented in them, which express certain relations of power; for example, any 'innocent' remark spoken by a man to a woman can be discursively read as having a sexist inflection - given the relations of power that obtain between the sexes.

This is where a 'determinist' position is often advanced, wherein such behaviour is seen to reflect the structural basis of society. Whilst I am in no doubt that, 'in the last instance', children's literature contributes to the reproduction of existing social relations (in the way that class, race and the sexes are depicted), such blanket pronouncements miss the dynamic ongoing accomplishment of this situation. My point is that within any textual weave there will always be certain threads which can be teased out - unpicked, even. Walkerdine (1990 pp. 10-11) provides an appropriate example. Some children, under supervision, were 'playing hospitals', such that the power of boys (doctors) over girls (nurses) was reproduced. However, one of the girls - Jane - used a Wendy House to change the discourse to one of domestic regulation, and in the process, successfully managed to challenge the doctor's control.

Now obviously this in itself reproduces existing relations, but simply to speak abstractly about power 'oppressing' is to miss what Foucault called 'its strategic resourcefulness, its positivity' (1979, p. 86), whereby the girl is empowered, making the situation signify differently. Yet this only works, not because of individual creativity, but because this discourse of domestic regulation already has an institutional siting. Hence Foucault's methodological injunction to look at discursive practices, at the capillary action of power, and not to invoke abstract notions of 'ideology' or 'patriarchy': themselves discursive constructs.

Besides Foucault's conception of discourse, I shall be using some related terms developed by Volosinov/Bakhtin (2), who also argues for the importance of studying language in use. Thus Bakhtin (1981) speaks of the 'heteroglossia' of texts, which is a useful shorthand for the weave of voices that constitute textuality, any of which discourses a reader may appropriate. It is in this process of taking up particular discourses that we develop ways of talking about ourselves and others. Discourses thus help define us, giving us an identity (in that we become the 'I's of certain discourses, the gendered beings of others), and ways of interpreting the world and its texts.

Unlike some other versions of this (e.g. Althusser's 'interpellation'), the process here is dynamic, in that we are not simply pawns of a monolithic ideology; instead, 'ideology' is actively negotiated in particular practices. Yet because it is an active process, this means that particular signs can be given a different 'accent' - as achieved by Jane above. Signs thus have specialised usages for particular social groups, plus a history of different usages. This makes for what Volosinov (1973) calls the 'multiaccentuality' of the sign. The word 'children', for example, varies widely in terms of the age range signified (Aries, 1973), and in terms of its discursive placing; it can equally signify 'natural innocence' or 'bestial corruption' (Robertson, 1976).

Finally, it should be noted that this view also breaks down the division between self and society, in that 'the word' is seen as 'the semiotic material of inner life - of consciousness' (Volosinov, 1973, p. 14). Hence, when talking about 'personal responses' to literature, these can only be communicated using discourses that precede the speaker - in effect, producing yet another text, another weave. As Vygotsky puts it, speaking about the whole developmental process: 'development in thinking is not from the individual to the socialized, but from the social to the individual' (1962, p. 20).

To recap: a discourse approach suggests that any topic must be seen in terms of the particular practices that constitute it. I shall look at children's literature in this light - in particular, at how it is positioned in relation to the powerful discourses of literature and education/ developmental psychology. These are powerful precisely because of their institutionalisation: their meanings are continually being reconstructed in educational settings. The term 'children' is particularly resilient here, institutionally defined not only by the human sciences, but also in discourses around the family, health and welfare.

After looking at how these institutions position children's literature, I then want to make space to explore children's own interpretations of a text they themselves selected (Dahl's **The Twits**). Again, using Foucault's lead, this will involve looking at a particular concrete practice, and attempting to see how a text can be productive for children, both in the discourses they bring to it and what they make from it.

This outlines the area of research, and the approach, but behind it, let me reiterate, there is my third concern, which is to attempt to demonstrate how a 'Communication Studies' approach might be fruitful in approaching children's literature - fruitful in giving children a voice without turning them into ideological pawns, or ciphers of particular developmental stages.

I shall now turn to the two main institutional bases of children's literature - in literature and education/developmental psychology - and spend the next two chapters examining the subject's positioning within each. This, in turn, will lead on to an examination of Dahl's **The Twits**, and children's discussions of it.

## Chapter 2 - The Literary Tradition

In this chapter I shall examine two literary approaches to children's literature: the text-based 'great tradition' approach most closely associated with F.R. Leavis (noting similarities with the arguments of the 'social critics'), and the more reader-centred position of Iser's 'Reader-Response' criticism. The latter, also closely associated with education, should provide a suitable bridge to chapter three, which specifically considers children's literature in relation to developmental psychology.

## The 'Great Tradition' and Its 'Lesser' Offspring

The term 'literature' did not always have its current connotations. As Williams (1976, pp. 150-4) points out, the terms 'literary' and 'literate' were once synonymous. However, since the seventeenth century the former has become increasingly evaluative, applicable to a progressively more exclusive range of texts. This re-definition was part of a much wider social process of nationalism and class-formation, but the salient point is that literature came to be seen as a preserver of values in a period of moral decay brought about by industrialisation (3). Certain texts were seen to transcend social divisions, achieving a harmony, a coherence, that might ennoble those who studied them (Baldick, 1983; Mulhern, 1979). However, an oppositional tradition has argued that this coherence is false, achieved only by excluding certain groups and areas of experience, and glossing over contradictions (Macherey, 1978). For example, **The Wind in the Willows** is celebrated for its arcadian depiction of a natural and ordered world (Inglis, 1981; Sale, 1978). However, others have indicated the uneasy tensions represented by the Wild Wood's inhabitants (Green, 1959; Carpenter, 1985; also Needle, 1981); yet another reading could point to the absence of women.

So, the sensitising role of great literature is in many ways insensitive: its discourses cohere most solidly and naturally around white, middle-class, adult, male heterosexuals. The further one moves from this centre, the more inhospitable the 'great tradition' looks. In terms of children's literature, its 'adult-centredness' is particularly evident amongst Leavisite critics. Though they write about children, they do so to celebrate values that only a small minority might appreciate - values, also, that they find in only a small percentage of the literature. Inglis is explicit on this, with his 'Lesser Great Tradition' (1981, p. 101), his opening sentence mirroring Leavis:

> The great children's novelists are Lewis Carroll, Rudyard Kipling, Frances Hodgson Burnett, Arthur Ransome, William Mayne, and Phillipa Pearce - to stop for the moment at that comparatively safe point on an uncertain list. (1981, p. 3)

These novelists, he argues, seek 'to transcend division and find a new unity of culture and being' (ibid., p. 117). Rustin & Rustin likewise speak of the 'truth-bearing quality' (1987, p. 2) of certain children's fiction, with its 'deep structure of meaning' (ibid., p. 26).

The Leavisite critics (4) seem to assume one of two things: either that children come to see the canon in the same way, because of its intrinsic qualities, drawing us 'beyond the narrow confines of the self' and encouraging 'a **love** of life and a disinterested sense of the beauty of all living things' (Hall, 1983); or, that the children do not really matter, for the books are great in themselves: 'The evidence is not in what the books **do** to children ... but in what they **are** in themselves' (Inglis 1981, p. 74). As C. S. Lewis put it: 'I am almost inclined to set it up as a canon that a children's story which is enjoyed only by children is a bad children's story' (1969, p.210).

Thus, whereas the child-oriented critics (discussed later) argue that 'a [children's] book which is not read by children cannot be considered good' (Huck & Young, 1966, p. 15), the literary critics argue the opposite: '**Tom's Midnight Garden** and **Puck of Pook's Hill** are wonderful books whoever you are, and that judgement stands whether or not your child can make head or tail of them' (Inglis, 1981, p. 7). This is a defensible position, but has little to do with children: it is for adults, as Inglis appears to confess: '[it] revives in us the childlike qualities of freshness and innocence and delight' (ibid., also cf. Cott, 1984).

Before moving on, there is another group of critics who believe equally in the power of literature to affect us, albeit they hold very different values. These 'social critics' also believe that literature can be 'bludgeoning and beguiling', to use Whitehead's Leavisite phrase (1986, p. 56) and that we should therefore protect children from it (Dixon, 1977; Klein, 1985; Leeson, 1985; Stones, 1983). Thus in the **'Spare Rib' List of Non-sexist Children's Books**, Lindgren's **Pippi Longstocking** is commended for its positive female image, with the caveat: 'but use this book with care - chapter 9, **Pippi goes to a tea party** is to be avoided for its racist remarks about Black skin colour' (Stones & Mann, 1979, p. 12).

The text is still all-powerful here, beguiling our children - even those of 'Spare Rib' readers! - regardless. As with the Leavisites, it is adults who know better, marginalising child views, and helping construct children as helpless innocents. Thus Writers & Readers (1979) can list nine pointers to help detect 'racism and sexism in children's books', not one of which involves consulting children (the nearest is a hypothetical, 'Consider the Effects on a Child', p. 144).

Yet presumably these critics were themselves readers when young. Inglis (1981) in fact, confesses to having enjoyed Sapper and W. E. Johns. Did the social critics never read Lindgren and Blyton? Ray's research suggests otherwise, in that many academic high achievers read the latter (1982, p. 91), and the lesbian critic Hennegan has specifically celebrated reading Blyton amidst Dostoevsky and Flaubert (1988, p. 175) (5). Why is it only others that are seen to be at risk? Whilst these critics' writings discursively construct the child as a passive and defenseless innocent, they themselves seem to have been immune. This elitism, combined with the way the child is constructed, seems to obviate a need for empirical work, which is remarkably absent amongst both literary and social critics.

With this in mind, I should now like to move on to a second literary approach, one that presumes to give the reader more of a voice.

## 'Reader-Response' - A Bridge Between Literature and Children

In this section I shall briefly outline Iser's version of Reader-Response, which seems to be one of the most favoured in talking about literature and children (Chambers, 1985; Corcoran & Evans, 1987). However, I shall suggest that despite its avowed commitment to bringing in the reader, this occurs neither in theory nor practice.

As the term suggests, reader-response was welcomed for the way it moved away from the centrality of the text, which 'affected' the reader (like 'direct effects' research in media studies), to seeing the reader as a more active maker of meaning, under the guidance of the text (similar to 'Uses and Gratifications' in media work). Texts, Iser argues, contain 'blanks' or 'indeterminacies', which readers actively bridge, thus constructing their own sense.

Nevertheless, though readers are active, the extent of their freedom is dubious, for the text is said to construct an 'implied reader' through its 'network of response-inviting structures'. Good readers are those who are open and responsive to this construction. Yet, if we successfully respond to such textual instructions, are we not simply at the mercy of the text? Iser thinks not, in that readers bring different background experiences to bear. However, in the way he describes the effective reader, it is clear that it is these very background experiences that we are meant to put aside, in order to be receptive to the text. In other words, we are meant to be active, but not over-active! As Eagleton (1983, p. 79) points out, this suggests that good readers should not hold too dearly to particular values. Yet, if they are held lightly, are they worth much anyway? Furthermore, if we are so open to change, is literature really special? How is it superior to other texts - to political speech or soap-opera?

Here we can detect an implicit liberal humanism (Leavis was simply more explicit). Theoretically we are all active readers, yet there seem to be 'correct' readings which the text implies for us. As Gilbert (1987) infers, the 'implied reader' is actually an acutely refined reader, from which most of us fall short. When allied with a 'personal growth' model, which it frequently is, there is the idea that these texts will help us become - of our own volition - similarly sensitive, rational beings.

Aside from this theoretical confusion, reader-response also has limitations in practice. Firstly, it does not actually seem to widen the canon much. The traditional texts continue to dominate, which tend to be those encoding the values of the dominant culture. Purves (1973) in a study of ten countries, found this to be the case in all of them: each saw literature as a way of enculturing its young into the ways of the dominant ideology, however that might vary across countries. Other studies have shown that the children's books considered the most important are those that celebrate the values of individualism, and of cultural majorities (Glastonbury, 1980; Shannon, 1987) and are not always the ones preferred by children (Hill, 1989).

Secondly, even given a wider range of reading, there are other problems. One is the school context: pupils are aware that texts are in school for didactic purposes. Medway (1980), for instance, in an experiment giving children more autonomy in their learning, noted how children suddenly became more receptive to texts they had previously disliked. This is not in any way to blame teachers, who are caught up in the same system, as Protherough admits: 'there is an apparent gulf between the responses teachers say they value and wish to encourage and those which much of their work and most of their examining processes actually elicit' (Protherough, 1983, p. 8).

Thirdly, there is the problem of 'closure' in Iser: the way texts are 'tamed and subdued to some firm structure of sense' (Eagleton, 1983, p. 81). The question here is 'whose sense?', for Iser's work leaves out all political and social questions in the production of a text. Hence the active closing of blanks might gloss over the very things that Macherey argues should be opened up. In a classroom context, the identification that some readers might experience in reading **Huckleberry Finn** might marginalise others (Klein, 1985, p. 45). It seems that the dominant meanings are always going to be the ones towards which class discussion centres, and there is some sensitive research showing that children are socialised from the beginning to realise that only certain meanings are appropriate to bring to the classroom (Baker & Freabody, 1989b).

This leads to a related point, which is that, irrespective of the different social and cultural backgrounds of children, schools have their own discursive practices, in which children's literature is situated. Children learn that 'personal response' does not exactly mean what it says: it does not mean relating the text to last night's television, for instance; rather, it seems to involve filtering one's reactions through a peculiarly literary register. In short, much of the process is precisely learning to 'do lessons'; that is, to keep things going by filling the 'blanks' appropriately (to borrow Iser's terminology), often regardless of personal investment or comprehension (e.g. Edwards & Mercer, 1987; Mehan, 1979).

To illustrate what I mean I would like to finish this section by looking at children's reactions to Kemp's **The Turbulent Term of Tyke Tyler** (1977) - a book frequently commended for its positive image of a girl (Dixon, 1982; Stones, 1985). In reading it, most people assume (though there are hints) that the robust hero is a boy until the end, when Tyke is revealed to be 'Theodora'.

I was interested to hear that it was a class reader in my 12 year old son's form. From discreet questioning, he seemed to be enjoying the book. However, when I next mentioned it, the book was damned outright as "rubbish". Indeed, it was hard to get beyond this epithet; he seemed genuinely outraged. If, as Jameson (1975) claims, a 'genre' forms a contract between writer and reader, then my son felt that this book had welched on him. His sexism seemed more virulent than ever, and he is now more wary of books that might be in any way novel (6)!

However, according to his class teacher, my son had apparently shown a sensitive awareness to the gender implications of the book. This latter reaction matches Jackson's research, where he discusses the book's ending with four pupils, two boys and two girls. Jackson adopts Iser's approach, arguing for the book's ability to 'provoke the active participation of the reader in having to repair these gaps in understanding' (1983, p. 64), and he purports to show how the stereotyping is challenged, and the role models for girls expanded.

Of course, it can be argued that my son is experiencing this educational process, which simply takes an extended period of time to manifest itself (Peters, 1966). However, a discourse explanation seems to fit his reactions far better. Thus, in the classroom, he used the appropriate register, helping to keep the lesson going, but outside school another discourse prevailed. Girls, of course, might find the book more encouraging, yet the problem remains. For girls are in any case required to read more books featuring boys, and thus learn how to understand 'the male' in preparation for their later role in life. They boys do not have to do this, sitting more 'naturally' in adult discourses as the 'he' which is the norm: it is only discourses specifically about women that require explicit gender marking. **Tyke Tyler** challenges this, certainly, but for most of the tale it seems that the boys enjoy a good read, whilst the girls are learning again about boys and their supposedly typical interests. This interpretation is given added weight by Moss (1989, p. 6) who, when she introduced her secondary pupils to it, found that many already knew it; however, they remembered Tyke as a boy. As she says, 'the ending had washed over them'.

To sum up: I have suggested that Iser's 'implied reader', though 'he' affects to stand for all, in fact represents a particular class, gender and ethnicity. However it is the position around which the discourses of a text 'most naturally' cohere. Thus, when Iser commends the reader who is open, putting aside preconceptions, he is tacitly endorsing very particular preconceptions, supportive of the status quo. Rather than the text coming to the reader, the reader is meant to surrender to the text, abandoning a 'personal' response for the position of 'implied reader' in a particular literary discourse.

Reader-response criticism therefore ends up in many ways similar to the Leavisite position. But whereas the latter is openly elitist, reader-response affects a more democratic approach, such that readers of their own volition produce acceptable readings. In Foucauldian terms, this can be read as an example of the capillary penetration of power, such that it 'reaches into the very grain of individuals ... inserts itself into their actions and attitudes, their discourses, learning processes and everyday lives' (1980, p. 39). In other words, there is no need for Leavis's missionary zeal: people themselves come to think in these terms, of literature enriching and transforming them (as in the Bullock Report, 1974). What one is transformed into, or how one is richer, is seldom questioned; nonetheless, these chains of signification around the idea of enrichment effortlessly help us construct our talk about literature, about education and about development in general.

Given this powerful way of speaking, many of the social critics reconstruct the same subject positions, although they hold very different values. Accordingly, children are read as either the helpless victims of bad literature, or the beneficiaries of the good. The children themselves are rarely heard - hardly surprising if one is positioned as being helpless and impressionable: they would know no better. Yet, as I have tried to show with **Tyke Tyler**, children are not simply pawns. 'Good' literature will not necessarily improve them, nor, as I shall try to show later, will a 'disgusting book' (Rees, 1988, speaking about Dahl's **The Twits**) harm them.

In order to do this, however, we need to restore the marginalised child. Yet this is unlikely to occur at these powerful sites which cohere round adult centres of culture. They, after all, keep children's literature marginalised, in that so little of it is seen to meet their criteria. Thus Shavit's dream of placing children's literature in the forefront of literary scholarship (as quoted on p.6) seems unlikely, but if it were to occur, I suggest it would result in the literature being further removed from children.

In concluding this section, I want to emphasise that though these discourses about 'growth through literature' have powerful institutional sites, they are by no means confined to them. They circulate widely in society, through the media, by eminent people quoting key texts, and of course, through schooling, providing us with the very terms by which we think about the subject. To probe this more thoroughly, I shall now turn to see how 'growth' and 'children's literatureὂare entwined in the discursive threads of educational/developmental psychology.

---

## Chapter 3 - Children, Psychology and Literature

The literary critic needs the psychologist, Schlager declares, throwing down the gauntlet, because 'the "magic" which lures children [to particular books] relates directly to child development' (1978, p. 142). She adopts a Piagetian framework, which is the most common stance taken by psychologists involved in children's literature. In this section I shall look briefly at Piaget's work, then in more detail at two examples of Piagetian criticism, Schlager's and Tucker's, the second intending to show the limitations more generally of a specifically cognitive approach.

Piaget's influence is massive, in fact hard to avoid as a discourse on children's literature. Even those not explicitly wedded to his approach adopt his developmental terms, seeing literature as concerned with cognitive development (e.g. Margery Fisher's children's literature journal, aptly named **Growing Point**).

However there are serious problems with Piaget's work, which I shall briefly outline, to point up the contrast with the approach taken here. Firstly, there is his individualistic conception of development - of an isolated cognitive being acting on the world, rather than a social being growing through interaction with others. Secondly, there is his neglect of language in this process. For Piaget, language simply clothes underlying thoughts, rather than helps shape them, and, in the process, helps shape us. Thirdly, his notion of across-the-board stages of development is increasingly questionable (e.g. Brown & Desforges, 1979): many now see development occurring in a far more incremental way, and occurring in more context-specific areas (which is more in line with a discourse approach). Fourthly, the notion that these stages climax in a 'Logical Operations' Man is increasingly suspect (Gilligan, 1982; Walkerdine, 1984; Wason & Johnson-Laird, 1977). Lastly, there is the criticism that, despite a bold stand against a reductionist behaviourism, Piaget himself underestimated children's abilities in many areas (7).

I shall elaborate on this last point, as it has a particular bearing on my approach. Matthews' work (1980; 1984) is very useful here, incisively showing how Piaget missed various chances to explore children's versions of events, preferring simply to read them as lacking when measured against the objectivity of adult rationality - which, as Matthews also points out, Piaget seldom questioned. Thus, using the Piagetian method, Matthews shows that such thinkers as Plato and J.B. Watson might also be accused of operating at the stage of 'concrete operations', given their notion of thinking being inner speech (Matthews, 1980, pp. 42-43).

There are three points I want to draw from Matthews' work. Firstly, he shows that Piaget is wrong to assume that children will have nothing philosophically interesting to say simply because they are meant to be operating at a different developmental stage. Matthews manages to take children's responses seriously without essentialising childhood in this way. Secondly, he contends that stories are a particularly good vehicle for exploring ideas, in that they proffer virtual or 'as if' worlds (ibid., pp. 56-66; also Bruner, 1986).

Lastly, though Matthews does not express himself in these terms, I think his reading of Piaget shows the contextual nature of our utterances. In other words, that they are discursively situated. They cannot be applied abstractly, but have a particular domain of relevance, which, as Foucault argues, is held in place by relations of power. Thus children may be read as 'egocentric', or 'concrete' thinkers or believers in 'imminent justice'; however, adults rarely are, despite similar signifiers. To give an example from children's literature, McDowell (1976), drawing on Piaget, argues that children's fiction is distinctive in being more active, more dialogue based, morally more clear-cut, and less rational than adult fiction. But his examples of the latter - Joyce, L.P. Hartley, etc - clearly show that his discourse is constructed round a fairly narrow literary tradition, ignoring that large part of adult fiction which is just as morally clear-cut, full of action and dialogue, and not overly rational.

I should now like to move away from Piaget himself, and turn to a fairly typical appropriation of his work by Schlager. As quoted in the opening to this section, she sees a developmental approach as the magic key to understanding children's literature, irrespective of cross-cultural differences:

> whereas people may be culturally different, the biological aspects of human growth do not vary much from one nation to another or from one culture to another. We are dealing with a universality among children. (Schlager, 1978, p. 137)

Schlager expresses herself poorly here. It is tautologically true that biological aspects are fairly invariant. However, stories, their language and values, exist in the cultural realm, where there exists a great deal of local difference - as I shall show later.

Schlager's case is based on analysing Newbery award winners for signifiers of the concrete operations stage, characteristic of 7-12 year olds, and correlating this information with library circulation figures. She claims that those stories which best exhibited the concrete stage of development were borrowed most. However, there are several queries to raise. Firstly, she has delimited her research to adult approved books, which are not those most popularly selected by children. What of the characteristics of these other books that children may more readily 'clamor for' (ibid., p. 142)? Secondly, her data do not tell her who actually borrowed these books - simply that some circulated more than others. She is presuming that these books were borrowed by 7-12 year olds, rather than, for example, adults. Thirdly, even presuming this age group were the borrowers, we do not know that they actually read the books. It may have been other factors that appealed, such as cover picture, use of illustration, chapter layout, or size of print. Lastly, the ˙ problems of Piaget's own inferences from his conversations with children have already been mentioned, but these must pale beside the task of determining the stage of development of a book: Schlager concentrates on the behaviour of the main character, but why this rather than the book's literary qualities - the theme, use of imagery or irony - which, it might be argued, require more advanced, logical abilities? After all, it should be remembered that these books were specifically **literary** award winners. Hence, it might be more apposite to ask why the books appeal so particularly to literary adults - presumably like Shavit.

Moving from Schlager to Tucker, we find a much more circumspect critic: 'We can discuss some purely cognitive, intellectual limitations that most children have at some ages that do apply to books' (Tucker, 1976, p. 179). Nevertheless, although Tucker is not so bold about the 'magic' of a developmental approach, his work is actually further removed from readers than is Schlager's. He tends to conduct **post hoc** analyses of why certain books have appealed, organising his chapters in line with Piagetian stage divisions. However, it is the general lack of 'ecological validity' that I wish to criticise here, the way that he makes general claims about children and books from often tenuously connected experimental situations.

I have taken one instance to demonstrate the limitations of this approach, as against a more contextually sensitive stance. Thus, in arguing for simplicity of language and plot, Tucker quotes as evidence just one experiment, which showed that 59% of 7 year olds misinterpreted the sentence 'The girl standing beside the lady had a blue dress'. However, when the embedded clause was presented separately, almost all understood it without problems (Tucker, 1981, pp. 13-14). My criticism of this work is that books or stories do not feature at all. If one wants to look at how children read and understand books, it seems one should observe children doing just that. Accordingly, I replicated the original study, adding a condition where the syntactically complex sentences appeared in the context of a story. I found that whereas the solitary sentences still caused problems, those in the story did not (see Appendix 1).

Yet my aim is not to set a new, more correct, bottom age on these competencies. Rather, I am arguing that their truth is dependent on context - on the discursive frame within which they are produced. Vygotsky's work seems particularly useful here, seeing human activities as 'tools' which help transform us. He saw the mastery of signs in this way: 'the child's intellectual growth is contingent on his mastering the social means of thought, that is, language' (Vygotsky, 1962, p. 51). It is thus misguided to speak in terms of age-bound cognitive competence; rather, he suggested, we should address the potential - the 'zone of proximal development' as he termed it - which the culture can amplify. Fiction, I suggest, can be seen in this way, not in a restricted cognitive sense, but as generally providing a focus for the development of particular discursive powers.

Lee provides a useful example of this. He found that his British Jamaican students thoroughly enjoyed a novel that was, in literary terms, 'trite and probably worthless' (Lee, 1984, p. 234), and in social terms, explicitly racist (a white's tale of ignorant black slaves under the sway of African black magic). However, as Lee shows, the pupils engaged with the discourse on Jamaica and blackness, effectively empowering their own writing.

So, whilst I am in no doubt that children develop, I question Piaget's structuralist account of it. It would seem that, apart from possible maturational factors of attention span and memory capacity, a growing experience of various discourse repertoires gives a perfectly adequate account of the process. It links the social to the personal, avoiding the attempt to posit a biological climbing-frame for what seem social processes - a biological frame, it should be noted, that places Western man at the pinnacle of creation.

In a discourse approach there is no such universal, privileged vantage point: all knowledge is culturally dependent, discursively situated. Thus, in the West, students in higher education will learn the discourses of particular subjects, but their knowledge will still be 'embedded'. In this way, we find that in some contexts adults will be read as 'concrete thinkers', whereas in others, children will be seen to exhibit abstract reasoning (Brown & Desforges, 1979). Finally, this approach breaks down the restrictive notion of 'cognition': discourses circulate concerning mathematics, certainly, but there are also discourses about what Piaget disparagingly refers to as 'mere romancing' (1951, p.10). What the latter lack, of course, is institutional support. But Piaget, as Matthews notes, seemed only to be concerned with officially sanctioned knowledge.

We can now more fruitfully question Schlager's attempt to bypass culture and ground the appreciation of story in biology. For it seems that her conception simply reproduces the dominant middle-class view, both in terms of structure and content. This was the view, in fact, that Heath (1983) found amongst her white middle-class community, 'Maintown', where life revolved round print, such that the discourses of books quite closely matched their 'extra-textual' experience. Heath contrasts this cultural norm with two other communities' conceptions. Here I shall just mention one - black, working-class 'Trackton' - where stories were also plentiful, but oral rather than book-based. The stories were also much more open and pervasive, drawing extensively on everyday life. There were not the official openings and closings; like soaps, they lacked formal coherence. They were also being continually reworked, making fantastic originally realistic events, with a stress on excess, on colourful language and violent content. Miller similarly found more worldly-wise tales told in Baltimore ghettoes (Bruner, 1990, p 83), and nearer home, Steedman (1982) recorded a 2,000 word story written by three 8-year-old, working-class girls which also mixes a fairly harsh realism (of sex, poverty and poor housing) with fantasy.

These alternative versions of story should make us realise that the 'purely cognitive' inevitably has a social dimension. The 'truths' about children's needs and interests are themselves discursively constructed, albeit they have real enough consequences. However, these notions become so natural, tied into institutionally sustained truths about 'childhood' and its 'stages', that they prove difficult to rethink, until challenged (cf. Walkerdine, 1984). Thus, a recent picture-book story by Pirani (1988) seems to have qualities in common with the stories of Trackton and Baltimore. It depicts a girl defending her sandcastle against aggressors (assertively, with a sharp tongue, rather than violently, whilst her father dozes nearby (she does not wake him to be rescued). This empowering tale obviously challenged adult notions of childhood and its literature, arousing fifty-four MPs to object to it (Sandberg, 1989)!

Whilst content is probably the most sensitive index of what is appropriate (or not) in children's literature, 'truths' are also circulated about other requirements; as, for example, that the literature warrants a special language, which should be simple and transparent; that below about 6/7 years of age children cannot distinguish fiction from reality, and that children prefer simple uncluttered illustrations of whole figures (8).

The constructedness of this 'normality' is perhaps best demonstrated in surveys of children's reading, where it is found, for instance, that amongst pre-adolescent boys war books/comics are very popular. But this is not an innocent fact: war stories are predominantly about male characters engaging in traditionally male-related pursuits - ones that are endlessly celebrated as desirable by the media. However, the key question is, would this truth still obtain if the works featured women in war - as Resistance Fighters, for instance? No doubt my son, for one, would change his reading habits.

When these child-centred critics come to explain
the incredible popularity of writers like Blyton and
Dahl, a stage explanation is once again readily
invoked, stressing their extreme simplicity of
language and plot. This often seems like a slight
on both writer and reader. Thus Tucker (1981, p.
106) gives voice to the belief that 'if children were
capable of writing novels, they would write like
Enid Blyton' (Steedman's work, above, might cast
some doubt on this). It is worth noting how
frequently this tactic is used by the dominant
culture to denigrate others. Early male critics of
the women's novel made very similar remarks:
'...as a form easy to write and possessed of no
traditional technique, it could be dashed off by any
lady' (J.T.Taylor, quoted in Lovell, 1987, p. 9).

However, before going on to suggest that it is in
social terms, rather than the 'purely cognitive',
that these writers can be seen to be of significance,
I shall try to draw out the main threads of my
argument in broader terms.

I have suggested that both literary and
education/psychologically-oriented critics seem
united in their celebration of lone individuals,
developing through their own actions on the
world. Books are seen to aid this process of moral
and cognitive development. Essentially it is seen
as a movement from inner-being outwards,
eventuating in an autonomous, rational, yet
morally sensitive individual. Thus, through 'his'
own constructive activity, the individual comes to
be at one with the logic of the world. And being at

one, 'he' goes unnoticed, 'his' constructedness becoming the norm; hence 'he' can unproblematically stand as a gender-neutral pronoun - in that the discourses of the world are constructed with 'him' at their centre. For him, the world is coherent; others diverge from this norm.

I have also argued that this notion needs standing on its head (or rather, its feet): that this normality is actually a discursive achievement, albeit massively supported at various institutional sites. Hence, rather than an inside-outwards movement, development proceeds outwards-in, the social always predating the individual, giving him/her the semiotic material of social existence. There is, consequently, no place to stand outside discourse. The rational man, who **uses** language, rather than it using him, is a myth. As I tried to show earlier, the paragon celebrated by all these critics turns out to be gendered (not a 'he' above gender), coloured (white also being a colour - not purity personified), and class-located. Finally, and significantly, s/he is also adult, which, I have argued, is not synonymous with being logical, dispassionate, and objective; consequently, children should not be read as though defective in relation to some ideologically constructed adult norm.

It should now be clear why the discourses of literary studies and developmental psychology marginalise children's literature, for their centres cohere elsewhere. It should also be clearer why those critics who are interested in children's literature, themselves being part of these discourses, seek to improve its status within their discipline's confines, rather than

looking elsewhere (Shavit and Schlager, above).
In this way, however, its lowly status is
reproduced, for the very reason that these
discourses cohere around adult meanings. Hence
my argument for an approach which gives more
space for children to respond; for children to
demonstrate the nature of what, in terms of the
above institutional confines, can only be read as
'in-coherence'.

Putting this into practice, I would now like to turn
to one of the books that some children actually did
'clamor for' - Roald Dahl's **The Twits**, the subject
of the next chapter.

## Chapter 4 - Dahl and 'The Twits' - An Analysis

The Twits (Dahl, 1982) emerged as the chosen work after a class of 8-9 year olds at a local school were asked to nominate their favourite book. Given its dubious standing amongst critics, this suited my purposes admirably. I have divided this part of my work into three sections. The first deals with critical reaction to **The Twits**, the second tries to tease out the various discourses in the work, and the third looks at how children themselves discuss it. Throughout, I shall attempt to develop an approach which keeps the book in a cultural context.

## Dahl, The Critics, and 'The Twits'

Many adult critics seem genuinely surprised that, given so much 'better' material around, children persist with Dahl. Some suggest that his work appeals to children 'who are over-trained, over-clean and over-organized: children who seem to be starved of the sort of earthy humour which is childhood's own' (Butler, 1986, p. 146). (What, I wonder, does Butler make of adults who like Rabelais and Swift?) Nevertheless, the key point is that there is a lack here of any attempt to consult children. In fact some think it wise not to draw children's attention to this sort of work (Landsberg, 1988; Townsend, 1976). And some, following this precept, do not. Trelease's **The Read-aloud handbook** (1984), for instance, mentions none of Dahl's three most contentious works: **The Twits, The Witches,** and **George's Marvellous Medicine.**

Searching the main reviewing journals for reaction to **The Twits**, Margery Fisher's **Growing Point** also appeared to ignore it completely. The **TES** (Anon,

1980) simply reproduces an illustration from the book, together with a few anonymous lines summarising the plot (unfortunately the caption reads 'Portrait of an anti-heroine', but the picture is of **Mr** Twit: very much an anti-heroine!). In **The School Librarian,** Churchill declares that 'the first three chapters, devoted to expounding the obscenity of Twit and his beard, are entirely nasty' (Churchill, 1981).

Of critics who have written more generally about Dahl, again, the majority seem hostile (e.g. Cameron, 1972, 1978; Itzin, 1985; Landsberg, 1988; Rees, 1988). Brampton (1986) and Landsberg (1988) draw attention to his supposed misogyny, and Itzin (1985) declares that 'womanhatred is at the core of Dahl's writing'; indeed, she goes on to link boys' reading him with committing gang rape: 'they could as easily be Roald Dahl readers as watchers of video pornography and violence'; in reading **The Witches** 'boys learn to become men who hate and harm women'. For Itzin, the text seems to reign supreme, whilst girl readers seem invisible - again reproducing the social norms mentioned in the last chapter.

Haigh (1981) describes **The Twits** as 'Dahl at his most outrageous...the only children's book I have ever read which has literally made my gorge rise' (although his review is generally positive). Rees terms it 'a disgusting book', 'facial hair is perceived almost as a moral defect: bearded people are dirty and are trying to hide their real appearance'. He goes on, 'Do we want them ['relatively young children'] to think that all ugly people are evil, that all physically attractive people are virtuous? (1988, pp. 146-7).

I have left out the accusations of racism here, most apparent in **Charlie and the Chocolate Factory**, but also made of his other works (e.g. **The BFG** - Gill, 1989; Klein, 1985). Nevertheless, the point has been made: there is a considerable disparity between child and adult views, although there seems little communication between the two camps.

**'The Twits' - A Textual Study**

Texts, as I have suggested above, do not possess some underlying meaning or essence which an author has managed to encode in a particular arrangement of words, themselves 'implying' a reader who can reconstruct, or decode the text. Instead, I have argued that a text is a weave of codes, or discourses, which readers will find meaningful in different ways, depending on their personal experiences, their knowledge of other stories, and their socio-cultural background. Though these three areas are analytically separated here, from what I have said about the word being 'the semiotic material of inner life - of consciousness' (Volosinov, 1973, p. 14), it should be clear that the concept of discourse unites all three, in that even personal knowledge is conceptualised discursively (i.e. one must speak, for example, in terms of 'personal abuse', 'sadistic treatment' or 'just punishment' - categories which pre-exist the speaker who mobilises them).

Drawing on literary, structuralist and psychoanalytic work, I shall attempt here to pick out various discourses in **The Twits** that I think readers may draw on in 'making sense'. In a later section we shall then see what discourses readers do indeed mobilise. First, though, a summary of the story.

Mr and Mrs Twit are a repulsive couple who continually play mean tricks on one another. They live in a windowless house and cultivate a garden of weeds. They were once circus people, and are trying to train a family of monkeys - the father, Muggle-Wump, being the only named one - whom they keep caged in the garden. They want the monkeys to perform an act where they do everything·upside down. Mr Twit has a penchant for bird pie, the birds for which he captures once a week by spreading 'Hugtight' glue on a dead tree's branches. Regrettably, Muggle-Wump cannot warn the birds, as he does not speak English. However, the Roly-Poly bird - a friend of Muggle-Wump from Africa - arrives on holiday. A firm believer in learning the languages of the countries he visits, he is able to warn the birds. He also helps the monkeys escape and together, both monkeys and birds avenge themselves on the Twits, using the glue to invert the Twits'·house, and, as a consequence, the Twits themselves, who come, literally, to a sticky end!

The story is tersely told over eighty-six pages, which are divided into twenty-nine short sections, illustrated on almost every page. However, short sections and illustrations describe most children's books. It is the way these are utilised that contributes to The Twits' success; for each section has a title, broadly indicative of the content, yet is also, in terms of Barthes' 'hermeneutic code', a generator of suspense (e.g. 'Mr Twit gets a horrible shock'). Thus, whilst most sections recap the events of the previous ones in a fairly restrictive way (e.g. one ends 'Mrs Twit began to feel so trembly she had to sit down', the next begins 'As soon as Mrs Twit sat down...', pp. 30-31), the section titles throw the text open to the reader to make predictions. Quentin Blake's illustrations perform a similar function, in that they are positioned so as to depict action before it is textually described.

In this way the story works well as a 'psycholinguistic guessing-game' (Goodman & Goodman, 1977), whereby reading is seen not as a passive decoding process, but as a meaning-making activity: people read by bringing their existing knowledge (or appropriate discourses) to a text, from which they make predictions, which are then confirmed (or not). Texts which are successful in this way not only empower their consumers as readers, but also help them see themselves in various discursive acts. Again, this accords with Vygotsky's work, in that the book can be seen as a useful tool for developing discursive knowledge.

Another helpful organisational feature is the way the text gradually increases in complexity. It begins with short tit-for-tat reversals (glass-eye in beer/frog in bed), which, once understood, become more involved, with the 'dreaded shrinks' and stretching episodes. Not only this, but the plot in these earlier sections is 'paratactic' - that is, one reversal follows another, co-ordinately; there is no superordinate structuring. Such plots are easier to comprehend than 'hypotactic' ones. However, eventually Dahl draws these paratactic events into a more complex hypotactic structure, thus giving the plot a logical denouement:

Twits glue birds ———— Birds glue Twits

Twits invert
monkeys ———— Monkeys invert Twits

Hoax 'dreaded
shrinks' ———— Actual 'dreaded shrinks'

Thus Dahl not only shows inversion in the content, but demonstrates it in the story's structure, too.

The inversion of order seems to be one of the two main themes in the book, and I shall return to it below after discussing the other, the use and abuse of power (10). This is a recurring theme in Dahl's work (e.g. Mrs Trunchbull in **Matilda**, Lancaster in **Danny**), which Dahl himself relates to his childhood, suffering indiscriminate beatings from sadistic masters and prefects (Dahl, 1986). Being the butt of the arbitrary exercise of power is no doubt something that most children can relate to - whether it be from parents, teachers, peers, siblings, or strangers.

For almost the first half of the book Mr and Mrs Twit are shown trying to outdo each other in various devious ways. No other characters feature at all. There then follow four chapters which show that the Twits' power is exercised on others too, in a selfish and unacceptable way: their caging of the monkey family, making them perform tasks upside-down, their weekly capturing of the birds using superglue, and the incidental capture of four boys, whom Mr Twit seems quite prepared to eat. Finally this indiscriminate power is overthrown, but not, it should be noted, by physical force. As in most of Dahl's books, he shows that power is of two kinds - physical and 'brain power' (as Matilda's ability is described). Though the smaller and weaker characters are oppressed by physical power, they eventually triumph through their exercise of brain power (usually seen as an innate quality) - as in Muggle-Wump's 'brilliant idea' (Dahl, 1982, p. 68).

Regarding the inversion of order theme, many theorists have pointed to the significance of this for testing reality: boundaries have to be transgressed in order that the borderline be better known. Thus do we construct and reconstruct reality, separating it from fantasy, from mere appearance (Douglas, 1966; Jackson, 1981). Those things which do not fit neatly into cultural categories consequently develop a particular potency, in that they resist 'order': as Douglas puts it, dirt is 'matter out of place' (1966, p. 12), which is what the Twits - especially Mr - present to us. Douglas' mentor here, Levi-Strauss, has made much of the mixture of fascination and revulsion that attends those things which confuse the Natural and the Cultural.

The Twits encapsulate several contradictions. First, there is Mr Twit's dirty hairiness, linking him to nature rather than culture, and specifically to the monkeys (who are rightfully hairy). On the other hand, he tries to turn monkeys from their natural state into cultural beings, to have them 'dress up in human clothes and to smoke pipes' (Dahl, 1982, p. 52). The Twits also encroach on bird behaviour: Mr Twit eats worms, thanks to his wife, whilst she is seen to fly - an anomaly which the birds explicitly come to watch. Lastly, the garden's one tree - a dead one - is made to bear fruit weekly; yet the crop is birds, which are plucked, unnaturally, like fruit. All these features play on the confusion of categories, broadly along the Nature/Culture divide. It is for this reason that the more natural (i.e. categorically apposite) 'bare' boys and Fred the gasman feature. They are truly 'human', providing a contrast to the naturally 'animal' birds and monkeys.

The Twits are also ambivalent in terms of age. In some of their behaviour they appear childlike, with their practical jokes, their messy eating, their not washing; yet their appearance signifies maturity: the beard, the walking stick, and the hairiness. Duffy (1972) in her psychoanalytical reading of fairy stories, points to the sexual connotations of hairiness - as in dwarves, wolves, Bluebeard and Pan - and as recently re-accented by Carter (1990). Mr Twit's hair is described in terms that connote the pubic: spiky and bristly. The 'pilosi' or hairy ones, who loved to play tricks, were also traditionally brown in colour - as is Mr Twit on the cover of the book - where he is seen carrying his beloved 'Hugtight' glue, a sticky substance with fairly obvious seminal overtones! Moreover, at the end, when their power is overcome, they are seen to shrink - or detumesce. Then there is Mr Twit's general oral fixation (his drinking and eating), which is frequently linked with sexual devouring (he threatens to eat the boys he finds in the tree). Finally, let us not forget the classic Freudian symbols of male and female, the tree and the house, which feature extensively.

Unlike Bettelheim (1976), Duffy (1972), or Rustin & Rustin (1987) who take these things more literally, I must emphasise again that I am not offering the above as the underlying meaning of the story. My point is simply that such discourses are continually circulated 'as interpretations' by our culture. They are ready-forged chains of signification which easily lead us along these paths. A second crucial point is that texts 'signify' rather than 'reflect' or 'encode'. Just as I criticised the Piagetians for presuming that certain signifiers always index the same underlying competence, so I am critical of those like the Rustins when they make a statement such as 'wand = penis' (1987, p. 93). They presume to have struck bedrock rather than developed an interestingly potent discourse by giving signs a particular inflexion. Crudely, this psychoanalytic discourse allows one to accent any protuberance as 'penis', any concavity as 'vagina'. As I suggested above, the potency of this discourse can be socially located, arising out of the way we categorise our world. Sex accrues power because it focuses on the way the 'natural' erupts within the 'cultural'. Such meaning can be repressed, but so long as culture is ordered in a certain way, it will continue to be discursively potent, attracting symbolic resonances.

Returning to **The Twits** then, I am suggesting that the very things that repulse some critics, such as Rees ('a disgusting book'), are precisely what give it power. They are also the things that should ensure that children will not take the story literally, contrary to Rees: 'Do we want them ['relatively young children'] to think that all ugly people are evil, that all physically attractive people are virtuous? (ibid., pp. 146-7). Whereas a more naturalistic protrait might be confused, this story's excess guarantees its unreality. In other words, the story is itself likely to clarify notions of culture v nature, of sense v nonsense. Part of the delight comes, then, from seeing how the mischievous couple are themselves 'twitted' by appearances: Mrs Twit thinking she is smaller because she seems so in relation to her stick; both Mr and Mrs Twit thinking they must be upside down, because their house seems to be so. Children's pleasure would be precisely in appreciating the difference between appearance and reality - unlike the gullible Twits.

Having dealt with the structure of the tale, and its two main themes, which, I have suggested, might partly explain its appeal, I would now like to explore it for issues of sex and class. In terms of the sexes, though Mr Twit seems to be the leader, Mrs Twit establishes herself as an equally active force. It is Muggle-Wump's wife who is more inert. She is the only character in the book who does not speak, whereas Muggle-Wump has much to say (11), and in many respects seems as autocratic as Mr Twit - "I'll stick **you** on to the ceiling if you don't shut up!", he declares (p. 75). Given that the male Roly-Poly bird is also active, there is certainly a male bias here. Moreover, traditional gender-roles are observed, with Mr Twit doing the 'hunting', and Mrs Twit the domestic chores of cooking and shopping.

What about class markers? Mr Twit seems vaguely lower class, though there are few overt markers: his bottled beer, perhaps, and the fact that the couple once worked in a circus (12). However, the audio-tape is more overt (Dahl, 1987), having the Twits speak in working-class voices. Yet there seems to be more to it than this, which I find most keenly captured in Bourdieu. He contrasts 'those who are "only natural" ' with 'those whose capacity to dominate their own biological nature affirms their legitimate claim to dominate social nature'. Because of this the underdog will seek to 'invert the relationship...using obscenity or scatology to turn arsy-versy, head over heels, all the 'values' in which the dominant groups project and recognise their sublimity' (1984, p. 491). It may well be that children find this aspect particularly appealing.

To draw this together: I have suggested that there are various discourses woven into **The Twits**. This should not be taken to mean that Dahl, as master weaver, is aware of them all. Although he may have refashioned them, these discourses pre-existed him. Moreover, particular readers are likely to exist in a different discursive relation to the text, depending on their socio-cultural, personal, and intertextual knowledge. Which areas they find significant (i.e. make signify) may therefore vary - as we shall see.

I have discussed the notion of physical power, as exercised by the strong over the weak, be they animal or human. However, this is counterposed to mental power, in which the physically weak can outwit (or out-twit) their aggressors. I have also suggested that the work explores various cultural/natural categories: adult v child, dirt/sex v innocence, and sense v nonsense. Though these are explored in what might be seen as a subversive way, it should be noted that Dahl generally reinforces institutional apparatuses: thus Muggle-Wump is presented as part of a family, whereas the Twits transgress this and other norms: they lack children, are not a loving husband and wife, and Mr Twit has no proper job.

Before I finish this section, I want it to be clear that this is not a mechanical process I am depicting. Meanings are not simply 'read off' if one has the right 'cultural capital'; rather, they are constructed, for books are also part of culture - are where, in fact, meanings are made. This was discussed earlier in relation to Vygotsky's work, and in the experiment with the syntactically complex sentences (Appendix I). Just so, **The Twits** draws on knowledge of birds roosting, of migration, of national and linguistic divisions, and so forth. But it might well be that, given their context in the story, less informed readers end up making more sense of these issues.

Finally, I am well aware that a Piagetian might point to other issues: the 'Immanent justice' level of morality, with The Twits being repaid in kind; or to Mrs Twit's 'conservation' difficulties, only measuring herself against her stick, not other reference points. They might point to the inconsistencies in the tale, in that Muggle-Wump can understand Mr Twit's English, but not that of others; or that the light-fitting and doorway would clearly show the Twits that their room was not really upside-down. Yet I have found that few adults notice these inconsistencies either. Readers, whether young or old, do not generally try to undermine their enjoyment. Just so, moving a top hat round a board in a game of Monopoly does not necessarily make one animistic!

**Dahl, 'The Twits',
and Children**

This section is based on my visits to three schools: **Cloverdale**, a predominantly middle-class village primary school, where **The Twits** was first nominated by 8-9 year olds; **Clogburn**, a Victorian, inner-city primary, with predominantly working-class children, about one-third Asian; and finally, **Sprawldon** - a secondary school, situated amidst urban sprawl, with predominantly working-class pupils (70% Asian). The pupils in the primary schools were mostly 8-9 year olds, those in the secondary were 11-12 year olds, though the latter had similar reading ages to the chronological ages of the primary children.

With the cooperation of the teachers, I managed to collect some written information on reading tastes, some drawings of episodes in **The Twits**, and to conduct some loosely-structured interviews with groups of children (in fours). With the Clogburn children, most of whom did not know **The Twits** beforehand, I was also able to arrange for them to hear half of the book (the part featuring the Twits alone) then to draw and write about the consequences before hearing the rest of the book, and discussing it. Full details of my methods, together with the quantitative findings, and selected transcripts and drawings, are to be found in Appendices II - V.

I shall now try to tease out the main discursive threads that emerged from the interviews, supplemented by data from written work and drawings. Despite my overt intervention, this will always necessitate trying to locate the material in a social context, not treat 'booktalk' as something separate. For this reason, literary critics might see much of the following as irrelevant. My point is to argue that, for the children, it is not: this is where they make meanings, and I am interested in what it is they make those meanings out of. I have organised the material so that it moves from general considerations about books to focus more specifically on The Twits.

The first point to note is that reading involves much more than cognitive or literary competence. Reading is a social activity: it both draws on cultural knowledge and is a site for the production of cultural meanings. Hence the importance for many of the children of 'seeing oneself as a

**Reading as a social activity**

reader' (Fry, 1985). This might mean owning, or at least knowing about, certain books/authors/characters. Tracy, at Clogburn, most clearly demonstrated this when I questioned her about her favourite author. She said she liked Blyton's books best, "Because they have small writing and I like to read small writing". After further conversation, in which she named 'Secret Seven' as her favourites, it emerged that she hadn't read any of Blyton's works at all: she simply liked the image of being a grown-up reader, reading books with small print (#1)[*].

In Cloverdale, where books were more prevalent, Blyton's status was less secure. Instead of advanced reading, her work might signify 'babyishness' - a common condemnation for works that had been well-liked at one time, and, in the case of Blyton, might still be listed privately as favourites. However, in mixed company, there seemed to be a reticence amongst the girls to mention her, and a total ban amongst the boys (she is also absent from the boys' list of favourite titles, though she emerged as their second favourite author!)

Dahl, on the other hand, was much more confidently named. In one Cloverdale group, I tried to draw out Sarah, a quiet, shy girl who liked Blyton. The others, Claire in particular, were quite outspoken in attacking Blyton, though their reasons were feeble. Blyton was first accused of writing babyish stories, then of using

[*]    # Refers to numbered transcripts, Appendix IV

inappropriate names for her characters, of being old-fashioned, and finally, of not being funny (#2).

The Cloverdale children thrived on a print-based world similar to Heath's Maintown. Books for them were used to mark status. The teacher fought a non-stop battle trying to stop them ranking each other by the books they were on. For the Clogburn children it seemed enough to be seen to be a reader. Cloverdale children moved more effortlessly through this world, linking titles with authors, speaking of blurbs, and even about the process of writing - of authors correcting mistakes until their stories read right (#3).

When I asked the various groups what their parents thought of Dahl's books, all the Cloverdale children said their parents were keen, even to the extent of offering to buy any of his books as an incentive to reading. However, at Clogburn, at least three said their parents disliked his books, and several thought their parents would not know his work (including some Asians whose parents did not read English). In fact, it is significant that many of these children did not already know **The Twits**, although their average age was slightly higher (9.5 at Clogburn compared with 8.9 at Cloverdale).

The Dahl books which the Clogburn children did know and love were predominantly those introduced by their class teacher - which accounts for the huge popularity of the first three titles in Table 2[*]. Cloverdale, on the other hand (Table 1), shows less concentration but greater variety, with an average of 2.6 titles mentioned per pupil, in contrast to Clogburn's 1.9 (Table 3) (Cloverdale pupils had also read far more books in general - see Table 10). At the extreme, however, lies Sprawldon. Unfortunately, these students were only asked to write down their one favourite book, but even then, five of the fifteen could not name a single one (Table 7).

If seeing oneself as a reader was important for many, for one or two it was equally important to be seen not to be a reader. Dan, a boy whom it would be easy to stereotype by his adherence to working-class machismo, was most outspoken in this regard, continually distancing himself from the image of book reader: he liked sport and fighting; he wanted to be a Sumo wrestler. He claimed never to have been in a library and found the whole idea of talking about books boring - though hoped it would go on longer, for, as emerged later, it kept him out of the classroom! However, although he clearly derived **kudos** from this image, it is possible that he might later fall victim to it, along the lines suggested by Willis (1977).

[*]      All Tables referred to are to be found in Appendix III

Having said that Dan was keen not to be seen to be a reader, I now realise that this reveals my own prejudices, for he actually enjoyed books on sport and the martial arts - and comics (again, markers of status). What he disliked was that image of reading which seems to be perpetrated, counter-productively, by much of the literary world. In this, the intrinsic superiority of books is continually stressed, sealing them off from other cultural spheres. This comes across in many supposedly impartial accounts of research. Thus, after discussing television, Singer & Singer (1979) comment:

**Books and other media**

> We prefer for the growing child the image of a quiet moment at bedtime when an adult sits by the child's side to stretch its own imagination amid warm surroundings. (Quoted in Davies, 1989, p. 100)

Trelease (1984), in a popular guide for adults reading to children, devotes a whole chapter to denigrating television, calling it 'the direct opposite of reading' (p. 101): it 'overpowers and desensitizes ... whilst books heighten the reader's sense of sympathy' (p. 102). Winn criticises television too, linking it with modern children's writing. She speaks of 'the Golden Age of Innocence', when 'children read books about fairies and animals, or about other children engaged in the carefree pleasures of childhood (Winn, 1983, p. 61).

I think enough of this has been quoted to show how such 'gatekeepers' construct their discourse around a cosy middle-class image of childhood: the right books ensure this, with their 'promise of happiness' (Inglis, 1981), against which television signifies the debased culture, which might, according to Postman (1982), destroy childhood entirely.

In denigrating TV, however, they are immediately erecting a barrier, with the powerful defining what is acceptable. In this way, some of children's likes are defined as oppositional, 'subversive', and so become more attractive. What might be a more open flow of meaning from one medium to another is frowned upon, intertextual references generally being permitted only between books, to prevent any miscegenation (Westall, 1985, bemoans how many of his pupils' favourite books were media linked). Certainly, when I mentioned television the children became visibly and audibly more animated, the prospect of discussing it in school (apart from educational TV) being seemingly unusual (13).

Consequently, I would argue that if we are to give children's literature more space, we must, paradoxically, recognise the centrality of television; for it is from the latter that many children's meanings arise, informing books. Yet even this is a compromise (as I have come to realise): it is more sensible to see books as part of the media in general. This was how the children most easily discussed them. Thus they talked about books on television (either read, as on **Jackanory,** or dramatised), books derived from television (e.g. **Byker Grove**), videos and films of books (and vice-versa), audio-cassettes of books, computer games of books (some knew of **The Hobbit** through this), or computer-game influenced books (as in the 'fighting fantasy' works of Steve Jackson). Yet, from my discussions, this did not mean that the book was submerged - it was simply put in a different context. Hence, in discussing the film of **The Witches**, one group pointed out the differences in presentation, noting, for example, that the main character is named in the film, whereas the book is related anonymously in the first person (something I had not noticed, and have since checked!) (#4).

In general, I think we must recognise that many of these children are more media literate than are we, that they may even develop a more visually influenced form of discourse. Thus, whereas media critics speak of 'reading television', Dan spoke of 'seeing' a book; another child talked about 'the star' of a book; a third, expressing ignorance of a particular book, said she did not know 'that programme'.

**Sex Differences, Sexism ... and beyond**

I have already mentioned the status of Blyton. In Cloverdale, certainly, she seemed to be defined in the public domain as exclusively a girls' writer. Given that Blyton is often accused of giving boys the active, leading roles, this raises some pertinent questions. In only one group did I find an overall preference for Blyton over Dahl, and this was the one group with a preponderance of girls (3:1). Seeking to follow up the sex-stereotyping arguments, I therefore asked them who the leader of the Secret Seven was. Rebecca stated, "It's a boy". But whilst Matthew started talking about something else, Victoria, in a voice so quiet that I had to ask her to repeat herself, ventured, "I think the leader is a girl". None of the others contradicted this - and Matthew quietly led the conversation elsewhere (#5). After this surprising response, I asked a Sprawldon group who the leader was:

Deena:      Peter and Janet I think, is.
Sanjay:     Peter.
Zakir:      Peter.                                    (#6)

It seems to me that in the first group the girls, for whom Blyton was already a girls' writer, were attempting to give her work even more of a female accent. Victoria's comment was not corrected by the others, although I made her repeat it, and despite it contradicting Rebecca. In the second group, however, where Blyton was less exclusively a girls' writer, the Asian boys intervened. Note how Deena ends with a singular verb, as if 'Janet' is a risky afterthought. I had only one more instance of what Volosinov saw as the struggle over the sign. Here the girl, Emma, stated that she liked 'Georgina' from the 'Famous Five' best. William immediately 'corrected' this to 'George'. For Emma, though, it seemed important to stress that the character was a girl, despite having to use the character's own less preferred form of her name (#7).

So, whilst it is an undesirable fact that girls, ethnic minorities and other groups are either under-represented in children's literature, or portrayed stereotypically, from my observations this did not generally impede their enjoyment of these books. In other words, I am suggesting that children do not actually need a character in the text of the same gender, age, or ethnic origin. **Contra** some of the social critics, the reading process does not effect such knee-jerk responses; instead, it involves the active construction of a position from which a text makes sense: it is a discursive achievement. Only in this way, I would suggest, can we understand how two 12-year old Muslim boys (in separate groups) each named a Dahl heroine as their favourite character - whereas elsewhere their patriarchal attitudes were regarded as quite offensive. When I asked if it mattered about Matilda being a girl, Irfan responded:

| Irfan: | It doesn't, because it is by a man. |
| Ahmed: | Yeah. |
| Darren: | I'm not bothered who it's by... (#8) |

Darren, the white boy, was less concerned about this - at least, in an all male group. In the other group, Sanjay explained Sophie's appeal (from **The BFG**) in terms of her intelligence.

Sexism proved to be a discursive practice readily mobilised. In discussing **The Witches**, Claire, a bright, physically advanced, dominating girl, was reduced to speechlessness by Peter:

| DR: | Do you think **The Witches** is more of a boys' than a girls' book? |
| Claire: | I don't know, about- |
| Nicholas: | Both the same. |

| Peter: | Probably both because it's about witches, which are women, but the star of it's a boy. |
| DR: | What do you say about that ... Claire? |
| Claire: | Cheek! |
| DR: | What do you think then? Do you disagree with Peter then, or what? |
| Claire: | Well ... there is horrible male people as well ... |
| DR: | What - |
| Claire: | ... like the Twits and things. |
| DR: | Like who? |
| Claire: | Like, there's Mr Twit, there's all the horrible giants ... as well as all the horrible witches ... [voice dropping to whisper] which are really women... |

| Peter: | And there's George's granny. |
| Claire: | I know. |
| Nicholas: | Hmm [affirmative]. |
| Peter: | Like you Claire. |
| Nicholas: | [high pitched snigger] |
| Claire: | I'm only nine!                          (#9) |

Claire is then quiet. As the issue had been raised I asked her directly whether Dahl "gets more at women or at men".

| Claire: | Well ... giants aren't exactly men ... and witches aren't exactly ... [voice fades away completely]. |
| DR: | They - They aren't...? |
| Claire: | Well they're dressed up. |
| DR: | They're not actually women? |
| Claire: | Mhm [vaguely affirmative].          (#9) |

58

Claire, who was previously quite happy with Luke-as-hero, has been denied that position by Peter, who points to the fact that Luke = male, witches = female. Claire tries to retaliate, pointing to the nasty male characters (again, Mr Twit is elsewhere one of her favourites), but is outflanked by Peter, so changes tack, though now unsure of herself. For some reason she seems unwilling to state that the witches aren't really women - though the text itself supports this (14), and her textual knowledge is otherwise thorough. Given her physical maturity, I would suggest that she actually quite likes the female power that the witches hold out (her favourite Dahl character is the Grand High Witch; also, note her 'escape' phrase, "I'm only nine!" (15). Thus she will relinquish this position of female power only reluctantly, particularly as she is otherwise the most dominant of the group. However, this illustrates how powerful the discourse of sexism can be. Itzin's comments, therefore, seem misguided: it is certainly possible to read **The Witches** as a rapist's **vade mecum** - indeed, Itzin (1985) does just this. But such readings are discursive achievements: possible, but by no means obvious.

What seems more characteristic is the way that Dahl empowers children: it is not so much that girls are oppressed by his misogyny, as given a voice to explore the unequal power relations between themselves, categorised as 'children', and the adult world. This became apparent when I asked one group why adults might not approve of

Dahl and **The Twits**. "It is about two horrid grown ups", was the answer, provoking much merriment (#10).

My own first contact with Dahl's children's work is also of relevance here. At the time I had a beard. I was sitting with two 9 year old girls and the mother of one of them. In response to some light banter, one of the girls turned to the other and muttered something about 'Mr Twit', which they found hilarious. From that point on they took none of my conversation seriously. It was the mother who enlightened me about the 'hairy ones' with food stores in their beards. The extent of such empowering use of books in everyday life is obviously very hard to capture, even if children are continually 'miked up', as in Wells (1986) - but it is clearly relevant to the way in which books can prove valuable discursive resources, and how, in the process, a book's meanings become re-accented; that is, how they are connected to other discourses. In this case, like Jane in the Wendy House, these two girls successfully renegotiated our adult/child relationship.

**The Twits**

Table 1 shows the popularity of this book at Cloverdale. The Twits were also popular as characters - Mr Twit in particular (Table 8). In interview it emerged that it was the tricks that were best liked - a finding confirmed in their drawings (Table 11), where the tricks accounted for 47% of all topics drawn. If they found any part of the book 'boring', it was the denouement. They were very ambivalent about this, resenting the predictability of the way things came together, yet desirous that it should be so. Indeed, the books they most disliked were the ones that didn't end properly. An analogy might be found in a comic character like Dennis the Menace, who always ends up back in ideological harness, despite celebrating his subversion for most of the strip. Clearly readers hope each week that it will not end this way, yet the endings are necessary, otherwise subversion ceases to be meaningful.

It seems significant, therefore, that although the children knew some parts extremely well, quoting the text verbatim, the ending was less securely fixed in their minds. For example, only one group remembered Fred, a gasman who appears at the very end, and that group thought he was a postman (#11). Three groups thought the monkeys had been flown back to Africa, whereas, in the text, this is only mooted by the Roly-Poly bird. Yet another group thought it ended with the monkeys moving into the Twits' house. In effect, they had rounded off the story more completely.

Bartlett's (1932) conception of 'remembering' is pertinent here, in that he saw it as a process of reconstruction - not simply of re-running stored tapes. This seems to be what the children are doing, recreating the story in line with dominant social discourses (16). Thus they also 'remembered' Muggle-Wump having a son and a daughter, though the sex of the children is never mentioned. In their drawings too, several reduced the four boys to three (Appendix V), presumably following the prevailing 'rule of three' norm (Atkinson, 1984). More puzzlingly, it was assumed by five groups that the Roly-Poly bird was female (#13, 14, 15). I originally presumed that this was because birds are often seen as female (bird/chick = girl). On reflection, however, it seems more likely that he is seen as female as a counter to Muggle-Wump. Hence, though the monkey commands, he cannot do so without the help of the bird, who frees him, communicates his orders to the other birds, and offers to see them all safely home. In our society all these functions are marked as more typically female. Such a reading also gives the story more balance, these two characters serving as foils to the Twits.

The Twits, as noted above, were very popular characters - but there was some ambivalence, in that they were also (elicited separately) the most disliked (Table 9) (17). They were seen both as childlike (or animal-like) and adult. In their tricks they were like the former, but they were like adults in their appearance (the hairiness, walking-stick, and glass eye) and status (their age, being married and owning a house). Several children resolved this ambivalence quite ingeniously. One remarked that the couple were senile and in their second childhood, whilst another described them as "like stone-age people".

The beard/hairiness of Mr Twit was particularly ambivalent. The children were both fascinated and repelled at the idea of developing secondary hair, some denying that they would, others declaring they would get rid of it. However, a few liked the idea: "It means you're grown up". Though these comments were largely from boys (and Muslim boys too) it was interesting that the rest were actively giving non-verbal support, or dissent, to each view. Obviously this was a delicate issue, and I did not pursue it. But my recordings capture much of the tension surrounding the topic, released in laughter (#16). Also, it is worth noting that the Clogburn children, who had only heard the story up to where Mrs Twit goes 'Ballooning up', most frequently suggested she gain revenge by cutting off Mr .Twit's beard (see Appendix V - one [C1] even recommends using a chainsaw! Surely as good an example of symbolic castration as that performed by Delilah on Samson!).

Although I reject any **de facto** psychoanalytic interpretation, Dahl's toying with signifiers along this Natural/Cultural boundary certainly attracts readers. The problem in our society is that this is constructed as either 'sexual' - in adult, phallocentric terms - or as 'lavatorial' - thus typical of young children. Such an opposition misses the wider appeal of this material (witness Billy Connolly's worldwide success), though it is indicative of society's need to see children as asexual (Jackson, 1982). Aside from the hairiness, the scene with the bare-bottomed boys proved most popular (Table 11; also see Appendix V). It also aroused much hilarity in discussion, and led to an increased sensitivity to other potentially slippery signifiers. Thus Peter, in explaining why the Twits' house had no windows, quoted the following: "Because they didn't want any Tom Dick or Harry looking in," which, although said straightfaced, caused much hilarity (#17).

**Realism v Fantasy in The Twits**

The children certainly did not see the book as realistic, rejecting any notion that Dahl was making a general statement about beards; neither did they generally agree that ugly thoughts made you physically ugly, any more than good thoughts kept you pretty. Having said this, they were prepared to consider any of these ideas seriously. They pointed out the realistic parts of the text (e.g. birds perching in trees) and counterposed these with the fantastic (e.g. gluing furniture to the ceiling). Likewise, they spoke of people who did not wash, whose food got trapped in their beards. Others demonstrated to me how ugly thoughts might affect looks, complete with tight-lipped, cold-eyed expressions - in effect, using the signifiers (what Barthes terms the 'semic code') so commonly used both by actors and novelists to convey character.

Such instances seem to me to indicate how certain texts, as cultural products, can be useful to think with. Particular discourses are made salient, re-accented, embroidered, challenged, or whatever. It is the process that Vygotsky highlighted when he talked about the importance of mastering sign systems, and of how a culture can amplify thinking. Thus one Cloverdale group can be heard thinking through various issues on the borders of possibility: "I don't think birds could talk," says Gemma, to which Dan responds, "Parrots can"; George points out that "they don't understand the language" though. Dan considers this, but responds that he understands his cat's language, "because, like when she's in the kitchen miaowing, I have to give her some food" (#18).

Some issues, of course, are more real than others for particular social groups. Two of the working-class groups, when I asked them in what ways the Twits were like adults, cited the Twits' violent behaviour. This was particularly overt amongst an Asian group:

| | |
|---|---|
| DR: | Do you know many grown ups that behave like the Twits? |
| All: | Yeah. |
| DR: | You do! |
| Bushra: | Yeah. |
| Shital: | Yeah. |
| DR: | What sort of - what sort of things do they do? |
| Yusuf: | They hit you, the - ... sometimes - |
| Shital: | They hit you, they boss you around. |

(#19)

Following a non-committal response from me, Yusuf launched into a story about a man luring a boy to his house and killing him. After the group had endorsed that the Twits were like adults in this way, Shital took up the issue, her grammar deteriorating as she became excited:

| | |
|---|---|
| Shital: | The way they hit children, they shouldn't hit children. |
| DR: | Mmhm. No. Right. |
| Yusuf | No, I say no. I say no. |
| Shital: | You shouldn't hit childrens when they ... [this last part unfortunately erased] |

(#19)

65

Whether or not any of them had ever experienced violence, they were patently very concerned.

Obviously, one can argue that the working-class are closer to violence, and that it is more prevalent amongst them as a way of disciplining children (Newson and Newson, 1970). Abuse statistics also show that it is more common amongst the unemployed and those in poor conditions (Creighton and Owtram, n.d.). Moving to the particular case of the Muslims (three of this group were Muslim, one Hindu), the situation is much more delicate. Perhaps for obvious reasons, there is no research that I could discover which looked into family violence amongst this group. However, the 'experts' that I spoke to informed me that it was more prevalent amongst Muslims, extending on occasions to public beatings in the mosques.

Aside from a discourse on violence that two groups mobilised in discussing the text, there was one other interesting thread that the Asian group developed. This was the problem of communication where there are language barriers. Two spoke of the problems their parents and relatives experienced because they didn't speak much English. Asked whether it would be a good idea if we all spoke the same language, the English children said, "Yes, English," but one added that his Asian classmate might prefer to speak "whatever you speak" (#20).

This was said in good humour; however, given a different context, it is clear that a discourse on racism could easily be developed here. Although I had not considered it before, **The Twits** would certainly sustain a reading which saw the monkeys as black Africans (like slaves), who, because they neither spoke the language nor appreciated the climate, could be seen to be better off in their own country. In a context where racism was more overt, this book might become a contentious text. In fact I am surprised, given Dahl's track record on racism (Klein, 1985), that this idea has not been developed elsewhere. My point, as with Itzin, is that these are possible readings, but depend on particular discursive practices to be realised.

Though Dahl's books - particularly **The Twits** - cohere around various hegemonic discourses (of the family, of the male, of the mental over physical work, and, more generally, of Culture over Nature), I have also suggested that they are particularly rich in exploring the observe of these. In the above discussions, whilst the hegemonic discourses have informed the children's comments, so too have more counter-hegemonic ones.

**Concluding comments**

This is as one might expect taking a discourse approach, in that the text will not simply reflect a class society. On the one hand, certain discourses are likely to be so engrained that they provide the very terms for our thinking about topics: we constitute them in this way, yet, in the process, we are also being constituted, as the subjects of these topics. On the other hand, this situation is by no means irrevocable. Away from the various sites of power, other discourses are always being generated, making the sign always open to new accenting in any concrete situation. It will be useful here to indicate each of these practices in operation, starting with the reproduction of some of the more powerful discourses.

The Clogburn pupils are worth consideration here, in that having only heard the paratactic, trickery part of the text, they had to predict the outcome. Though they depicted a general tit-for-tat progression in trickery (Appendix V), they lacked the textual information to see the hypotactic structuring. However, many introduced their own framing, in line with prevailing discourses. Thus many had Mrs Twit 'clean up', or reform Mr Twit in some way, just as an adult might a child. In other words, even without textual support these children were drawing on various cultural practices to help constitute a more closed text.

If we turn back to their Cloverdale peers, we find here too, that even with the whole text, extra-textual knowledge can still prove more powerful. Certain parts were fairly systematically mis-remembered: the ending was more fully completed, the sex of one of the main characters (the Roly-Poly bird) was changed, and two others (Muggle-Wump's children) were assigned a gender. This occurred even down to small details, such as one child calling the Twits' Wednesday bird pie "Sunday dinner". Like the pupils who 'forgot' that Tyke was a girl, these powerful discourses literally 'inform' our thinking.

Listening to the children talking, we can see these discourses being continually interwoven. This is the process that Vygotsky talked of when he spoke of cultural objects helping to amplify our thinking. However, as I have also argued, this should not be seen in a limited 'cognitive' way: it is a much wider social process, of knowing how to mean within a culture: cognitive categories are inevitably social categories, not biological imperatives (to use Kantian terms). Dialogues such as that about the division between human and animal, as to which can talk, which understand (#18), are part of this process, the children here coming round to constitute a category of social animal - the pet - which straddles the animal/human divide, and is characterised by mutual understanding. This is the category that the Twits abuse and exploit.

However, **The Twits** is more than just a pot-pourri of cultural tit-bits. As I have argued, its very structure and organisation make it particularly attractive. As my earlier experiment with syntactically complex sentences embedded in a story context (Appendix I) showed, the form can make the content more meaningful. Dahl's weaving of the paratactic into an overall hypotactic frame is a skillful example, as is the use of chapter headings and the placing of the illustrations. On this last point, the Clogburn children were found to have no problems at all in predicting how the story would unfold, simply from looking at Quentin Blake's illustrations.

So far, I have spoken about the way that various powerful discourses in society are woven into the fabric of the story, and of how the children reconstituted these, often embroidering them in line with prevailing discursive practices. However, within this heteroglossia, there are other elements that they clearly enjoyed, which might work against the overall weave. It is these, I would argue, that make the story particularly satisfying for children. Though again, it needs stressing that these discourses only draw their power from the fact that they exist within a constraining frame (the point made with reference to Dennis the Menace, above).

One such potent thread in **The Twits** is the discourse around lavatorial/sexual meanings, where signifiers become slippery and unstable. Hairiness, dirt, and bare-bottoms assist this, such that 'innocent' names like 'Dick' prove disruptive, and beards become phallocentric symbols of power. Though these meanings are enclosed by the tale, they are never fully contained. They are the parts that the children return to most regularly, they are the parts regailed in everyday conversation, and they are the parts best remembered. They are also, from my own experience of being bearded, actively mobilised to good discursive effect! Another powerful signifier was the violence of Mr Twit, which was observed developing into an oppositional discourse about adult power over children.

However, what I want to make absolutely clear here is that this subversiveness is not in some way concealed in, or essential to the text. Commentators, I think, often make this error (e.g. Lurie, 1990; Opie and Opie, 1959; Sarland, 1983). Rather, meanings are made out of the textual signifiers, in line with discursive practices operating at large. Thus elements may be used subversively, but equally, they can be turned to reactionary ends. An obvious example is the way that Peter appropriated elements from the text to 'do sexism', as Wise and Stanley (1987) put it. There was also the question of language barriers, which might easily have been given a racist inflexion, though not here. Clogburn lays great emphasis on integration.

This said, there can be no doubt that Dahl's major success arises from the way he empowers children, frequently managing to override differences between sexes and races by setting children up as a category juxtaposed to adults. Blyton, who is also said to take the child's side, does this by creating a cosy, alternative world, whereas Dahl seems to address relations of power more directly (the animals v. the Twits, Matilda v. her parents/Miss Trunchbull, Luke v. the Witches). Turning the Piagetian telescope round, they, or rather 'we', the adults, can be seen to be just as capable of being egocentric, morally delimited, and obtusely 'concrete' in our thinking. It is this reversal that Dahl offers, empowering children in a world of violent and powerful adults. It is also what makes him the butt of criticism from both left and right, both of whom construct children as a point of helpless innocence, needing protection from the adult world. Dahl, similar to Pirani (above, p. 31) helps construct a more assertive position - which not only those with beards might have experienced!

## Chapter 5 - Conclusion

I began this study with a commitment to a 'Communication Studies' approach to the issue of Children's literature, using the key concept of discourse. I shall now review its success - as an approach in itself, as a way of explaining the marginalisation of children's literature, and as a way of giving children's views more space.

A Communication Studies approach was defined as one that respected the meanings produced by different members of society, in order to see how these meanings were produced, used, and circulated. It was seen to be particularly interested in why some meanings have more power to stick, and, conversely, why the meanings of others are less recognised, or even noticed at all. Children's literature was seen to be a prime case where the intended audience was conspicuously absent from the discourses about the subject. I therefore examined its discursive placing within literature and education/developmental psychology.

It was seen that both these areas effectively celebrated some endpoint, a place where discourses cohered, and in the process, became transparent. In the case of literature, this was the transcendent realm beyond debased social divisions. For the Leavisites, this realm is seen to be recoverable in certain selected texts; for reader-response theorists, the coherence becomes something that the readers can achieve for themselves, if they are open to the text's guiding hand. However, this openness was seen to be a shorthand for effacing one's social background in order to become the text's 'implied reader' - an everyman around which the discourses would once again cohere. This was demonstrated most readily in the way a male accented language is seen to represent all, such that language makes male meanings more 'naturally' and positively.

In the case of psychology, the endpoint was seen to be rational western man, at one with the logic of the cosmos, from which others are graded to the extent that they fall short. Women fall short to some extent, but children far moreso, and increasingly so the further away from adults they are positioned.

These norms, I have tried to indicate, produce very powerful discourses, such that children, for example, are always read in terms of 'becoming' rather than 'being'. The metaphors of personal growth, of transformation and of transcendence through literature penetrate our talk deeply, such that many social critics recycle the notion of children being 'affected' by texts. The texts must therefore be divided into those with good effects, (ennobling) and those with bad (debasing). Children are consequently positioned as impressionable and in need of protection. Ironically, it is girls who are often read as particularly susceptible, thus reproducing their positioning as 'weaker vessels'.

However, a discourse approach neither sees this as a reflection of the power structure of society, nor as a fact of life because one is at a more immature cognitive stage. Instead, such notions are seen to be actively held in place through daily practices, which, in fashioning coherence around a certain centre, position others as marginal.

These marginalised groups, of which children are one, will seek to make meanings that increase their power. It is my contention, therefore, that the established sites of children's literature can never develop a practice which centrally involves children, simply because their centres lie elsewhere. They are always looking for works with suitable values or that are suitable 'growing points'. Thus, in seeking literature that is **good** for the child, they effectively **lose** the child - for they have redefined her/him as something dependent, or illogical, therefore at the mercy of textual effects. However, as a discourse approach reads it, children - just like the rest of us - are active participants in a whole nexus of 'textual' meanings, books being only a small part of the weave.

Any approach which wishes to explore this must therefore avoid essentialising children; rather, it should seek to look at children's literature in concrete social contexts. Instead of hiving off 'children's literature', it should see how it becomes meaningful for its readers precisely by observing the discursive threads that connect it with other areas of children's cultural practice. Hopefully this is what I have demonstrated in a small way with Dahl's **The Twits**, though I am aware that I have only a partially focused snapshot.

In showing how the old centres cannot hold, I do not think that I am loosing anarchy upon the world. I am simply showing the partiality of those literary and education/psychological approaches which attempt to rank order children's books. Rather than an anarchic 'deconstruction', what I hope has emerged here is the continual process of 'reconstruction', in which a particular discursive element can develop its own sense of gravity: as it signifies, so it becomes significant, and so discourse seeks to inscribe it. Thus, for instance, we saw how Mr Twit's cruel treatment of animals and children developed a particular salience.

For the future, I think more studies are needed of the way children use literature to make meanings - studies which do not prejudge the suitability of particular texts, but let this emerge from children's own accounts. This said, I must end by expressing my awareness of the relationships of power in my own research, in that I too have been appropriating children's meanings and weaving them into my own text. It is only to be hoped that the threads can be used productively elsewhere (18).

---

**Notes**

1. There are several critics who stand behind my work, though I shall not have time to deal with their own work in detail. Rose's path-breaking study (1984) is full of insight, but finally flawed, I think. She argues that the whole enterprise of children's literature is impossible, given its adult control. Ultimately it is founded on the adult's

unspeakable desire for the child, hence the cruciality of keeping it innocent, both in language and content. As she puts it, 'children's fiction builds an image of the child inside the book...in order to secure the child who is outside the book' (1984, p. 2). However, though her focus is elsewhere, she effectively removes the 'child outside the book' entirely - it is not just passive but a textual epiphenomenon!

Leeson (1985) is a second reference point, also arguing for a more open, media related literature. However, he takes rather a technologically determinist view of how this will come to pass, besides an equally determinist view of the way literature affects us. This said, he also has proved most informative. Finally, Hunt (1991) has long been a champion of a more child-centred criticism.

2.   As will be clear, I am using the term 'literature' in a strategic, more egalitarian sense.

3.   Following their translator, Michael Holquist (cf Bakhtin, 1981), I am assuming that these are one and the same person.

4.   I am using the term 'Leavisite' in a very loose sense. The history is far more complex than this, particularly in the case of I.A. Richards, who not only helped make literature seem scientific for the Leavis camp, but was also a precursor of the largely American 'New Criticism' with its stress on exacting textual analysis, nothing else being important. Finally, Richards was also a precursor

of Reader-response criticism, in observing
how his students actually read poems.

5.  I should emphasise that Hennegan is not part of
    this debate. I simply quote her as an
    academic critic who can still see Blyton in a
    positive light.

6.  I originally intended a more thorough study of
    **Tyke Tyler**. However, by the time I was
    ready, the book had been finished, and totally
    dismissed by some of my would-be subjects!

7.  There is an increasing number of studies in this
    area. Key ones here are the following:
    Matthews (1980, 1984) on children's abstract
    thinking in general - discussed in my main
    text; Donaldson (1986) on explanations;
    Coles (1986) on children's political and
    ethical thinking; and Peterson & McCabe
    (1983) on young children's understanding of
    causality in narrative. More disruptive
    critiques have been made from a
    post-structuralist stance (e.g. Henriques et al.
    1984, especially the chapter by Walkerdine),
    which informs a lot of my own work.

8.  On the importance of clear, simple language,
    see Cass (1971) and Huck & Young (1966);
    Tucker (1981) has already been quoted. Fox
    (1986) and Rose (1984) are useful critiques -
    the former more empirical, the latter
    theoretical. Baker & Freebody (1989a) give a
    close textual analysis of the social categories

behind 'innocent' words in first readers. Applebee (1978) originated the research which is endlessly recycled about children not being able to distinguish stories from truth before the age of 6-7. However, he is far less precise than those who quote him (Tucker, 1981). I agree with Applebee that it largely depends on experience (a discourse approach would argue the same). However, talking to 5-6 year old pupils at Cloverdale I came to disagree with his simple exclusion of 'nonsense' from the category of story. Applebee maintains that being a simple inversion of the truth, nonesense does not count. The Cloverdale children, however, showed a much more subtle understanding than this nonsense/truth polarisation. Thus, on **Cinderella**, dancing balls were seen as real, but travelling to them in transformed pumpkins was not. The only stories that they categorically called true were those about Jesus.

Regarding illustrations, Cass (1971), Huck & Young (1966) and Tucker (1981) make these points. Crago & Crago (1983) show a very different picture with their daughter. This book, a close developmental account, challenges many 'stage' claims, giving a far more relativistic, contextual picture.

9. As some children later pointed out to me, the birds are also inverted - with their legs sticking straight up out of the pie! The text on the pretended 'dreaded shrinks' is repeated almost word-for-word later (Dahl, 1982, p. 32, 94-5).

10. I have only recently come across Sarland's work (1983) through Hunt (1991). Sarland's is the only other work I have found to give Dahl's work serious consideration, comparing it with Blyton. From similar cultural studies reference points, Sarland finds in both Blyton and Dahl the theme of 'making sense of the world'; and, specifically in Dahl, the theme of 'reversal of power'. However, his conclusion, particularly taken up by Hunt (1991, p. 190) - 'that children are remarkably competent at handling all sorts of technical devices of storytelling provided that the story is clearly of their culture, for them' (Sarland, 1983, p. 170) - I find still constrained by a literary approach. A communication studies 'discourse' approach, sets both these points - of technical competence, and of an 'oppositional culture' - in a wider framework. Thus narrative competence should be seen not only in literary terms, but as a product of children's sophistication with other media - particularly television; likewise, the notion of an 'oppositional culture' needs to be seen in terms of differing cross-cutting strands, some of which unite children, some divide them, by gender, ethnicity, class, and so on; sometimes these discursive strands signify subversively, sometimes in a very reactionary way. These points are considered in more detail later in my main text.

11. 'Muggle-Wump' sounds very similar to the term 'mugwump', used of someone of importance, frequently a boss, who strikes their own independent stance.

12. Regarding class, I asked the children what sort of job they thought Mr Twit would do. The majority immediately responded 'dustman', though some wits came up with 'hairdresser'.

13. Against these critics of the media, Ingham (1981, p. 230) found that her most avid readers also watched the most TV. However, Whitehead et al. (1977) found the opposite: those who watched more read less. Could more recent readers have learnt to handle TV better? Ingham says that her avid readers had developed the mental technique of doing both at once.

14. Dahl, 1983, p. 30: "You don't seem to understand that witches are not actually women at all...in actual fact, they are totally different animals"'.

15. The 'glamour' of witches has been more systematically articulated by various feminists, returning the positive accent to the term 'witch' as 'wisewoman' (wicca); cf. Daly's 'wickedary' (Daly, 1987).

16. I have left out the work on story-grammars mainly for reasons of space. Bartlett's work still seems the best in this area, in that it is more socially located. Though others recognise the influence of society on the stories made, there

seems no room for notions of power or ideology in their grammars.

17. At least three of the same children rated the Twits/Mr Twit as both favourite and most disliked (there may have been more - some of the responses were anonymous). However, I am far from suggesting a contradiction in this.

18. Given room, it would have been useful to look at the National Curriculum in relation to my findings - in particular the attempt to give Media Studies a place in English - to the chagrin of others (e.g. Dodsworth, 1991). The Cox Report lists five roles for English, the fifth sounding in line with much that I have argued for. A 'cultural analysis' view encourages 'a critical understanding of the world and cultural environment in which they live'; they 'should know about the processes by which meanings are conveyed, and...in which print and other media carry values' (Section 2.25, unpaged). How on earth this will be united with their 'cultural heritage' model (more reminiscent of Arnold and Leavis) remains to be seen!

## Appendix I - Comprehension of Syntactically Complex Sentences in The Context of a Story

Reid took ten syntactically difficult constructions from basal readers and had her subjects (average age 7.4) read them first in their original form, then in syntactically simplified versions, controlling for semantic complexity and sentence length. The subjects were then questioned about the sentences. She found that the complex forms caused substantial problems of comprehension, which the simplified versions reduced significantly. Reid's subjects were mostly working class, ranging in age from 6.10 - 7.9.

For my experiment, I took two of Reid's ten complex forms:

'The girl standing beside the lady had a blue dress.' This is the one quoted by Tucker (1981, p. 14), which 59% of the subjects misunderstood.

'Mother's dress was neither new nor pretty.' This was the most difficult of all Reid's sentence forms, misunderstood by more than 60%.

I hypothesised that children would find these constructions easier if they were set in the context of a 'real' story (i.e. not a basal reader). I found a suitable text in Bisset (1970, pp. 62-4), which I adapted and presented in the version on the accompanying sheet (reduced to half-size).

The revised sentences, syntactically identical, are:

a) The oak tree standing beside the cherry tree had magic powers.'

b) 'In future, Mr Smith was neither mean nor
   hairy.'

I initially tested these on a control group of ten
middle-class subjects (average age 7.3). However,
they all understood (a), and eight of them
understood (b), using 'yes/no' responses to
questions like 'Was Mr Smith mean?' With a
younger group (average age 6.8, ranging 6.5 -
6.11), Reid's errors were replicated, with 60%
misunderstanding both (a) and (b).

An experimental group of ten pupils from the
same class was then tested (average age 6.9, range
6.5 - 6.11), who were fairly closely matched to the
controls in Reading Age. Each of these was then
presented with the story, as on the accompanying
sheet. They were instructed to read the story
carefully, as they would be asked questions about
it. The first question, concerning sentence (a), was
asked as they were about to turn over to the next
page (the story was arranged as a booklet, to make
it more like a story in a book, and to provide a
standard point at which to ask the first question,
before the memory load was too great).

It was found that all subjects understood (b) in
context, and all but one understood (a). It would
therefore seem that despite a greater memory load
(in terms of bits of information), the story made
the material easier to understand. With sentence
(a) there is no contextual support, so I can only
surmise that the story format helped focus
attention (the title draws attention to the tree as a

key component, and the sentence immediately prior prepares the reader for the information). Normally, if the type of tree was mentioned at all, it would be mentioned more than once, but in this case, it was deliberately withheld.

In sentence (b) there is clearly much semantic support for a correct reading. It may be objected that the subjects still did not understand the syntactic form per se. My point is that forms do not exist in a vacuum, although Chomskyan influence led to an attempt to isolate them. From a pragmatics perspective, it is only through meaningful contexts that such forms become comprehensible.

This, I would suggest, is a Vygotskyan approach, in which development is fostered in a supportive environment. The story itself provides a scaffolding that makes such terms more easily comprehensible - just as Beatrix Potter made 'soporific' understandable by its contextual placing.

In a follow up experiment, particularly in view of the middle-class bias of my subjects, I tried the same story on a group of ten younger children (aged between 5.9 and 6.6, average age 6.1) again with ten controls. However, not enough of these were sufficiently good readers, so I decided to present the story orally, otherwise replicating conditions. The results, however, were similar: 70% comprehended sentence (a) in context, and all subjects understood sentence (b).

# The magic wishing tree

The sun shone on the all the trees at the bottom of the garden, but one of them was special! The oak tree standing beside the cherry tree had magic powers. The wind blew gently through its branches and the leaves whispered, "Wish - wish - wish."

Mr Smythe stamped his foot and said, "I wish..." but he didn't get any further, because the blackbird said, very quickly, "I wish Mr Smythe was good."

And Mr Smythe, who had just been going to say, "I wish all the children were on the moon," suddenly changed his mind, scratched his head, and said, "I wish all the children would come to tea this afternoon, and we'll have cakes and orange jelly and lemonade for tea. And I'll shave off my beard, stop selling soap and open a sweet shop instead. And I won't let anybody call me William Cadogan Smythe, I'll just be called Bill Smith. Hooray! Hooray! Hooray!" And in future, Mr Smith was neither mean nor hairy.

He turned three cartwheels and all the birds in the tree started to sing again. The sun shone, the wind blew gently through the branches of the tree, and the leaves whispered, "Wish - wish - wish."

Whoever stood beneath it and wished, would have their wish come true.

In the house next to the tree there lived a fat old man with a beard. His name was William Cadogan Smythe. He sold soap in a shop in the village; and he didn't like girls and boys.

One day he stood underneath the tree and said, "I wish all the girls and boys who live near me were on the moon."

As soon as he said it all the girls and boys were on the moon. It was very cold and lonely up there and some of the younger children began to cry. But it was too far away for their mothers to hear them.

As soon as the children had gone, all the birds in the tree stopped singing. A blackbird looked down at Mr Smythe and said, "I wish all the children were back again, so there!"

Mr Cadogan Smythe said, "I wish they were all on the moon."

And the blackbird said, "I wish they were all back again."

The children were getting very confused; they didn't know where they were.

Bissett, D (1970) Time and Again Stories,
London; Methuen

On my behalf, a local teacher at 'Cloverdale' asked the pupils to note their favourite author and their favourite character. **The Twits** emerged as the most popular book, and Mr Twit/The Twits, the most popular characters. Besides many having read it and/or having it read to them, they had all heard this book on audio-tape in the 'Book Corner' at some time during the term, though it was by no means their only tape, nor the most recent. At separate times the teacher also had the class draw their favourite scene from **The Twits** and asked them who their most disliked character was.

With this information I then arranged to come in and talk to children in groups of four. This was done in a separate room, as informally as possible, though a cassette-recorder was openly visible. I talked with four groups in this way, three with equal numbers of boys and girls, the fourth with three girls and one boy. The children were 8-9 year olds (average age = 8.9), apart from one group, which had included some 7 year olds. They were predominantly middle-class (using parental occupation as a criterion, unsatisfactory though this can be).

# Appendix II - Methods Used in Investigating Children's Understanding of 'The Twits'

| Group 1 | Group 2 | Group 3 | Group 4 |
|---------|---------|---------|---------|
| Sarah | Rebecca | Gemma | Emma |
| Claire | Emily | Anna | Sophie |
| Nicholas | Victoria | Dan | Duncan |
| Peter | Matthew | George | William |

Because of the rationale of my enquiry, I wanted the discussions to be as much as possible on the children's own terms, as this would seem most likely to have them 'make meanings'. Thus, though I had pre-prepared a list of questions they were not asked systematically. In general I tried to make my questions arise from the flow of their conversation. I realise that this is an ideal confounded by all the power relations that operate in setting up interviews, in being an adult, in standing alongside teachers in an educational context, and so on. Frequently the children dried up and deferred to me, in which case it seemed least artificial as an adult to acknowledge this and respond accordingly.

I was straightforward about my project - being interested in the books children liked to read - though did not mention Dahl at all. I also explained that I wanted to tape everything, which seemed to bother no one, this being a common classroom occurence. However, at the end, they did all want to hear themselves, which resulted in two portions of my data being erased! Making audible recordings generally proved a problem. Despite several dry runs, the end product in Cloverdale was very poor in places. I managed to obtain some better equipment for the Clogburn sessions, and the room was also far better acoustically. Short of having children miked up, I see no easy way round this.

I also tried to make a mental note of any significant non-verbal behaviour during the interviews, which I wrote up in conjunction with the tape immediately after. Though this was by no means systematically

done, I was often able to recall information -
mainly eye-contact - around particularly
interesting points - often supported on the tape by
laughter, raised or lowered voices, etc.

'Clogburn' is a Victorian built, inner-city primary,
with almost exclusively working-class pupils, one
third of whom were Asian. Their favourite author
was also Dahl, though few of them had read **The
Twits** (much of their reading depended on teacher
initiative). This gave me the chance of having the
class listen to only part of the book being read,
using the audio-cassette version (Dahl, 1987). I
could then have the pupils predict the
consequences, which were both drawn and written
about (see Appendix V for examples). Aside from
the data from the whole class, I interviewed five
groups of four, three before they had heard all the
story, two afterwards. With the former I went
through the rest of the book with them, seeing if
they would predict the plot from the text's
illustrations, and, failing that, the chapter
headings. The groups here were predominantly 9
year olds (average 9.5), of mixed sex, with one
group entirely Asians. As the names below make
clear, three individuals managed to appear in more
than one group! Given that this was not a
controlled experiment, I don't think this
compromises my findings.

| Group 5 | Group 6 | Group 7 | Group 8 | Group 9 |
|---------|---------|---------|---------|---------|
| Tracy   | Lindsay | Donna   | Mandy   | Fatima  |
| Karen   | Julie   | Mary    | Bushra  | Shital  |
| John    | Stuart  | Sandy   | Yusuf   | Bushra  |
| Daniel  | Simon   | Chris   | Sandy   | Yusuf   |

Lastly, I visited a secondary school in an overspill area of 'Sprawldon', with many social problems. The ethnic mix here was 30% white, 70% Asian. I obtained some data on the whole class, then talked with just nine pupils, aged 11-12, from an 'English' class of sixteen pupils. The Reading Age of these students averaged 8-9 years (using English material). One of these groups consisted of five boys, the other, mixed sex. I used this school initially when 'getting my bearings', so it is more peripheral to my general enquiry.

| Group 10 | Group 11 |
|----------|----------|
| Deena    | Irfan    |
| Danielle | Ahmed    |
| Sanjay   | Darren   |
| Zakir    | James    |

Quantitative information on all the pupils' reading habits and tastes is tabulated in Appendix III. This provided useful background information to put alongside the qualitative interviews. It also makes plain how both subject and researcher use interpretive procedures in making sense. Thus, on the one hand there is Tracy, whose favourite author is Blyton, whose favourite titles are 'Secret Seven' books, who

finally admits to me that she had read none of
Blyton's books (see main section). However, in
her eyes, Blyton **is** her favourite author. On the
other hand, I made an immediate assumption
about the number of 'classics' mentioned by
pupils. It was only later that I discovered that
many of these were 'Ladybird' versions.
Whitehead et al. (1977) in their massive survey,
seem to have made the same assumption, though
without realising their mistake. Clearly I am open
to many charges of interviewer-led bias, which I
admit must be present. However, I would plead
that it is rarely escaped in any interview situation.
And, as I have indicated above, even with more
'objective' methods of eliciting responses,
interpretation both of the question (by the subject)
and of the response (by the experimenter) is
always present (Cicourel, 1964). In my terms,
people bring their discursive knowledge to the
situation and produce particular forms of sense
within that situation. My intervention was
specifically aimed to see what sense emerged, and
I would contend that any significance it has stands
or falls on the fact that certain discourses were
forthcoming rather than others.

Aside from the interviews I also used drawings,
which provided information in a form other than
verbal. They proved useful in indicating salient
areas, although I cannot rule out some copying
(certain drawings are rather similar). There was
certainly no evidence of any difference in
drawings between middle and working class
groups, or between whites and Asians. However, I

am dubious of reading too much into them, for in line with the discourse approach I have suggested, drawings must be seen to have their own conventions, which, like language, tend to produce certain meanings rather than others. Thus they almost all drew the Twits' house with windows, though it has none, and when questioned, they confirmed it had none. Yet they drew the house so because that it is the way they draw houses. For similar reasons, many of the children gave the dead trees green foliage, and whenever guns were drawn, they were inevitably firing bullets, although this does not happen in the story. Gombrich (1977) expresses my views on this eloquently, avoiding a reductionist biological explanation. Referring to Egyptian art, he points out that we would be wrong to think they saw the world two-dimensionally, simply because they do not use modern conventions of perspective (Goodnow, 1977, makes much the same point).

I had also intended to use Kelly's Repertory Grid Technique to discover the constructs that children use in discussing books. However, after eliciting three constructs from Cloverdale pupils, I abandoned the exercise. This was for two practical reasons, and two conceptual. Practically, the 'triadic elicitation' process proved difficult. The children found it relatively easy to pair two items, but less easy to state why a third one was different. Several researchers simply turn the first construct into a negative, but this is presumptious. It may be that someone is trying to articulate a new construct; for example, I might pair two novels because they are both 'sad', yet rather than see the third as 'not sad', it might be thought 'life-affirming', or 'humorous', or 'cosy' - which are by no means synonymous. Some researchers, like Applebee (1978), simply present their subjects with ready-made constructs, but this seems to defeat the whole idea of the constructs being 'personal' - the property of the subject, not the researcher. The second practical problem emerges when the grid is formed, and these constructs are applied systematically to all the items. Again, the children found this not only difficult but artificial, making comments like "I didn't say that about this one".

This brings me on to the conceptual issues, for after working through three of these constructs it seemed to me that I was guilty of trying to appropriate and distort my subjects' responses - the very thing I sought to avoid with a Communication Studies approach. Secondly, I came to realise that the method was actually antipathetical to a discourse stance. My criticism is similar to that made of the Piagetian stance, in that though both presume active, constructive subjects, underlying 'and undermining this' is the assumption that people exhibit a conceptual unity in the way they construct the world. A discourse approach queries this, suggesting instead that the unity is a fiction, or, at most, a discursive achievement.

Having gathered all my material, whether in written, drawn, or interview form, I then set about looking for particular areas of interest. Sometimes these were regularities, at other times, they were exceptions - both of which can be productive.

Beyond this, I was depending on my own cultural knowledge and interests to guide my enquiry. As I have argued above, we are all the time engaged in interpretive work and trading on our membership of society, viewed from a particular perspective. However one researches, these facts do not seem to be avoided - even in supposedly 'objective' scientific work (Gilbert & Mulkay, 1987). Were I to put a label on the approach, it would be 'grounded theory' (Glaser & Strauss, 1967), informed by much recent feminist work on method, which recognises one's inevitable involvement (Stanley, 1990).

**Favourite Titles, Grouped by Main Author-Cloverdale**

**Appendix III-Quantitative Findings From School-based Enquiries**

**Table 1**

| Titles | Female | Male | Total |
|---|---|---|---|
| **R Dahl:** | | | |
| The Twits | 5 | 3 | 8 |
| Matilda | 3 | 2 | 5 |
| The BFG | 3 | 2 | 5 |
| The Witches | 3 | 2 | 5 |
| George's Marvellous Medicine | 3 | 1 | 4 |
| Fantastic Mr Fox | 1 | 1 | 2 |
| Charlie and the Chocolate Factory | 1 | 1 | 2 |
| Danny, the champion of the world | 1 | 1 | 2 |
| The Magic Finger | 1 | - | 1 |
| The Giraffe and Pelly and Me | 1 | - | 1 |
| | 22 | 13 | 35 |
| | | | |
| **E.Blyton:** | | | |
| "Famous Five" | 4 | - | 4 |
| Castle of Adventure | 3 | - | 3 |
| The Secret of Killimooin | 3 | - | 3 |
| Brer Rabbit Stories | 3 | - | 3 |
| Five on Kirren Island Again | 2 | - | 2 |
| Five go to Smuggler's Top | 2 | - | 2 |
| Secret Seven | 2 | - | 2 |
| The Magic Wishing Chair | 2 | - | 2 |
| + 11 titles one mention each | 11 | - | 11 |
| | 32 | - | 32 |

**Other titles:**

| | | | |
|---|---|---|---|
| Tom's Midnight Garden | 3 | 2 | 5 |
| Simon and the Witch | 3 | 2 | 5 |
| Alice in Wonderland | 3 | 1 | 4 |
| The Lion, the Witch and the Wardrobe | 2 | 1 | 3 |
| Flat Stanley | 2 | 1 | 3 |
| Byker Grove | 2 | 1 | 3 |
| The Hobbit | 1 | 1 | 2 |
| Charlotte's Web | 2 | - | 2 |
| Treasure Island | - | 2 | 2 |
| The Beano | - | 2 | 2 |
| The Dandy | - | 2 | 2 |
| Saddlebottom | 1 | 1 | 2 |
| "Banana Books" | 2 | - | 2 |
| + 11 titles one mention each | 9 | 2 | 11 |
| | 30 | 18 | 48 |
| Overall total | 84 | 31 | 115 |

n = 27 (17 female, 10 male)

**Favourite Titles, By Main Author - Clogburn**     **Table 2**

| Titles | Female | Male | Total |
|---|---|---|---|
| **R Dahl:** | | | |
| The BFG | 17 | 12 | 29 |
| Matilda | 12 | 7 | 19 |
| The Witches | 10 | 6 | 16 |
| Charlie and the Chocolate Factory | 5 | 2 | 7 |
| George's Marvellous Medicine | 3 | 2 | 5 |
| The Twits | 2 | 3 | 5 |
| Revolting Rhymes | 2 | 1 | 3 |
| Esio Trot | 1 | 1 | 2 |
| Dirty Beasts | 1 | 1 | 2 |
| The Magic Finger | 1 | - | 1 |
| Danny, the Champion of the World | - | 1 | 1 |
| | 60 | 41 | 101 |
| **E Blyton:** | | | |
| "Famous Five" | 1 | 1 | 2 |
| Secret Seven | 2 | - | 2 |
| Five go to Camp | 1 | 1 | 2 |
| Secret Seven Mystery | 1 | 1 | 2 |
| Well Done Secret Seven | 1 | - | 1 |
| Mr Pink Whistle | - | 1 | 1 |
| + 8 titles one mention each | 6 | 2 | 8 |
| | 14 | 4 | 18 |

**Other titles:**

| | | | |
|---|---|---|---|
| Stig of the Dump | 2 | 4 | 6 |
| Oliver Twist | 2 | 2 | 4 |
| Great Expectations | 1 | 1 | 2 |
| David Copperfield | - | 1 | 1 |
| The Magician's Nephew | - | 1 | 1 |
| The Silver Chair | 1 | - | 1 |
| The Last Battle | 1 | - | 1 |
| Island of the Lizard King | - | 1 | 1 |
| The Temple of Terror | - | 1 | 1 |
| The Forest of Doom | - | 1 | 1 |
| Alice in Wonderland | 2 | - | 2 |
| George Speaks | 1 | 1 | 2 |
| + 7 titles one mention each | 6 | 1 | 7 |
| | 25 | 17 | 42 |
| Overall Total | 99 | 62 | 161 |

n = 32 (19 female, 13 male)

| No. of Titles Mentioned By Each School Group | | | | | | **Table 3** |
|---|---|---|---|---|---|---|
| | Cloverdale | | | Clogburn | | |
| | Female | Male | Total | Female | Male | Total |
| No. | 49 | 21 | 70 | 34 | 26 | 60 |
| Average | 2.9 | 2.1 | 2.6 | 1.8 | 2.0 | 1.9 |

n = 27 (17 female, 10 male)    n = 32 (19 female, 13 male)

| Favourite Authors - Cloverdale | | | | | | | **Table 4** |
|---|---|---|---|---|---|---|---|
| Author | Female | | Male | | Total | | |
| | % | | % | | % | | |
| Dahl, Roald | 17 | 100 | 10 | 100 | 27 | 100 | |
| Blyton, Enid | 14 | 82.4 | 5 | 45.5 | 19 | 67.9 | |
| Barry, Mary Stuart | 9 | 52.9 | 2 | 18.2 | 11 | 39.3 | |
| Townson, Hazel | 8 | 47.1 | - | | 8 | 28.6 | |
| Tomlinson, Jill | 2 | 11.8 | 4 | 36.4 | 6 | 21.4 | |
| Potter, Beatrix | 4 | 23.6 | 1 | 9.1 | 5 | 17.9 | |
| Murphy, Jill | 1 | 5.9 | 2 | 18.2 | 3 | 10.7 | |
| Lewis, C.S. | 2 | 11.8 | 1 | 9.1 | 3 | 10.7 | |
| King-Smith, Dick | 2 | 11.8 | 1 | 9.1 | 3 | 10.7 | |
| Arkle, Phyllis | - | | 2 | 18.2 | 2 | 7.1 | |
| Bond, Michael | - | | 2 | 18.2 | 2 | 7.1 | |
| Joy, Margaret | 2 | 11.8 | - | | 2 | 7.1 | |
| Ross, Tony | 2 | 11.8 | - | | 2 | 7.1 | |
| + 16 authors | | | | | | | |
| one mention each | 11 | | 5 | | 16 | | |
| | 74 | | 35 | | 109 | | |

n = 27 (17 female, 10 male)

**Table 5**

**Favourite Authors - Clogburn**

| Author | Female | % | Male | % | Total | % |
|--------|--------|------|------|------|-------|------|
| Dahl, Roald | 18 | 94.7 | 13 | 100 | 31 | 96.9 |
| Blyton, Enid | 8 | 42.1 | 4 | 30.8 | 12 | 37.5 |
| Dickens, Charles | 7 | 36.8 | 6 | 46.2 | 13 | 40.6 |
| King, Clive | 3 | 15.8 | 5 | 38.5 | 8 | 25.0 |
| King-Smith, Dick | 3 | 15.8 | 2 | 15.4 | 5 | 15.6 |
| Lewis, C.S. | 1 | 5.3 | 1 | 7.7 | 2 | 6.25 |
| + 8 authors, one mention each | 6 | | 2 | | 8 | |
| | 46 | | 33 | | 79 | |

n = 32 (19 female, 13 male)

**Table 6**

**No. of Authors Mentioned**

| | Cloverdale | | | Clogburn | | |
|--------|--------|------|-------|--------|------|-------|
| | Female | Male | Total | Female | Male | Total |
| No. | 74 | 36 | 112 | 46 | 33 | 79 |
| Average | 4.4 | 3.6 | 4.1 | 2.4 | 2.5 | 2.5 |

n = 27(17 female, 10 male)    n = 32(19 female, 13 male)

| Favourite Author/title - Sprawldon | | | **Table 7** |
|---|---|---|---|
| | **Female** | **Male** | |
| **Dahl, Roald** | | | |
| The Twits | - | 3 | |
| The Witches | 2 | - | |
| BFG | - | 2 | |
| Matilda | 1 | - | |
| Charlie & the Chocolate Factory | - | 1 | |
| **Blyton, Enid** | | | |
| The Magic Wishing Chair | 1 | - | |
| 'Couldn't think of one' | 4 | 1 | |
| | 8 | 7 | |

n = 15 (8 female, 7 male)

N.B.   Not one of the titles held in common by girls and boys

| Favourite Characters In Books - Cloverdale | | | **Table 8** |
|---|---|---|---|
| | **Females** | **Males** | **Total** |
| Mr Twit | 2 | 2 | 4 |
| The Twits | 3 | 1 | 4 |
| BFG | 2 | 1 | 3 |
| Mrs Twit | 1 | 1 | 2 |
| Mr Pink Whistle | 2 | - | 2 |
| Dog in Secret Seven | 2 | - | 2 |
| Matilda | 2 | - | 2 |
| + 23 single mention | 16 | 7 | 23 |
| | 30 | 12 | 42 |

n = 27 (17 females, 10 males)

Table 9

**Most Disliked Characters In Books - Cloverdale**

| Character | No. of mentions |
|---|---|
| Mr Twit | 4 |
| Twits | 3 |
| Mrs Pepperpot | 3 |
| Mr Men | 3 |
| Dennis the Menace | 2 |
| + 12 one mention each | 12 |
| | 27 |

n = 27 (17 female, 10 male)

Table 10

**Average No. of Books Read Since Christmas (till end April)**

| Overall | Females | | | Males | | |
|---|---|---|---|---|---|---|
| | mean | range | median | mean | range | median |
| Cloverdale 29.2 | 34.2 | 17-60 | 31 | 20.7 | 4-36 | 20.5 |
| Clogburn 17.7 | 16.8 | 1-40 | 15 | 18.9 | 2-40 | 20 |

N.B. These figures are based on children's own 'guestimates', although the teachers were able to assess their credibility. Teachers also had records of any reading connected with school, which provided a check. However, many of the children have probably included material read to them, or even material seen on television (e.g. the C.S. Lewis books). For these reasons, I have not made too much of these findings, interesting though they look.

| Favourite Scenes From 'The Twits', as Drawn by Cloverdale Pupils | | | Table 11 |
|---|---|---|---|
| Description | Female | Male | Total |
| Bare-bottomed boys escaping tree | 6 | 3 | 9 |
| Worms in spaghetti | 5 | 3 | 8 |
| Twits upside-down | 3 | 3 | 6 |
| Glass eye in beer | 3 | - | 3 |
| Mrs Twit ballooning up | 3 | - | 3 |
| Roly-Poly warning birds | - | 2 | 2 |
| Mrs Twit has the shrinks | 1 | 1 | 2 |
| Frog in Mrs Twit's bed | - | 1 | 1 |
| Picture of Twits' house and tree | - | 1 | 1 |
| | 21 | 14 | 35 |

n = 27 (17 female, 10 male)

(N.B. Some drew more than one picture)

| Table 12 | Favourite Characters In 'The Twits' - Cloverdale |  |  |  |
|---|---|---|---|---|
|  | Character | Female | Male | Total |
|  | Mr Twit | 9 | 5 | 14 |
|  | Mrs Twit | 2 | 1 | 3 |
|  | The Twits | 4 | 1 | 5 |
|  | Muggle-Wump/ |  |  |  |
|  | Monkeys | 1 | 2 | 3 |
|  | Roly-Poly Bird | 1 | 1 | 2 |
|  |  | 17 | 10 | 27 |

n = 27 (17 female; 10 male)

## Appendix IV - Transcriptions of Excerpts from Taped Discussions

The following twenty transcriptions represent about 20 minutes selected from approximately 5 hours of taped conversations. The numbers on the excerpts relate to the numbers given in the main body of the text, prefixed. All the names of the children have been changed.

### 1. Donna and Enid Blyton (Clogburn, Group 5)

DR: Why do you like Enid Blyton best?

Tracey: ... Because they have small writing and I like to read small writing.

DR: Mmhm. Does that mean if her books were in big writing you wouldn't like them so much?

Tracey: ... Well, I'd like her but...I preshe- I prefer her to write in ...

DR:     Yes. Do you like the stories she writes as well? Which type of - she writes so many, which ones in particular do you like?

Tracey:     Secret Seven.

DR:     Secret Seven, right. Who's -

Tracey:     [interrupting, impetuous] I've got about ... six of them at home.

DR:     Have you! Who's - who's the leader of the Secret Seven? Do you remember?

Tracey:     [quieter, head down] I've not read them yet.

DR:     Oh, you've not read any of them. But you think you'll like them. Right. Have you read **any** Enid Blyton?

Tracey:     [shakes head, looking down]

DR:     No. You just think you'll ...you just like the look of it.

Tracey:     [nods]

## 2. Enid Blyton's writing attacked (Cloverdale, Group 1)

DR:     Why do you like Enid Blyton better? I'll just ask Sarah here.

Sarah:     Don't know.

DR:     Er...you don't know -

Claire:     Well she hated children, she still wrote books.

DR:     She hated children, did she?

Sarah:     Well, she's got exciting stories.

Claire:     She- well she- she reads- she rea- erm she writes erm stories about golliwogs that talk and teddies and dolls ...and things.

DR: Mmhm. Doesn't she write other ones, though? I mean, they're ones that younger children might like.

Claire: Yes she writes erm, Se- she writes Secret Seven and Famous Five...

Sarah: [Simult.] -cret Seven

DR: Which ones do you like?

Claire: But they all have names like Tom and Anne and things like that.

Peter: [Simult.] I like [indecipherable] and things like that.

Sarah: I like Famous Five.

DR: Erm, do you not like them because of their names?

Claire: No, things like that, it's old-fashioned.

...................................

Claire: Well they've got no fun in them, really.

Sarah: They have.

DR: You think they have, Sarah?

Sarah: Ye-

Claire: Well they're not like funny, they don't describe people and everything...

Nicholas: Like Roald Dahl describes things well.

Peter: [Simult.] Like George -

DR: You don't think she does?

Nicholas: Not really, not as good as Roald Dahl's.

DR: Do you think she's exciting- she writes exciting stories?

Claire: Well some ... but others are just about little elves and things.

DR: Mmhm. But those that aren't, you know, those like the Famous Five and Secret Seven. Do you think they're exciting?

Sarah: Yeah.

3. On how authors correct their work
   (Cloverdale, Group 1)

    Peter:    He probably wrote the story with
   windows, and then when he got to the
   end, probably [indistinguishable -
   overtalked]

    Claire:    'Cos the thing is, he doesn't want any
   Tom, Dick or Harry looking in.

    DR:    Do you think- Do you think writers
   often do that then, David?

    Peter:    Er, yeah.

    Claire:    Mmm.

    Peter:    Things like, you do little things like that,
   then later on in the story found out that
   it doesn't work, so you just like, go back,
   and change it.

4. Appreciating the differences between the
   video and the book in **The Witches**
   (Cloverdale, Group 1)

    DR:    What about- what about, in **The Witches**
   when erm, the boy in that, he's a mouse at
   the end. Did you hope he'd get back to be
   a boy, or are you not bothered about that?

    Claire:    He liked being a mouse, but, on the video
   it showed him changed back to being a boy
   at the end.

    DR:    Did he?

    Claire:    Yeah.

    Peter:    Yeah.

DR: You mean on the film that's at the cinema? The one that's at the cinema - is that the same as the video?

Claire: Think so.

DR: 'Cos at the end of that I-

Peter: I saw it at the cinema - he was changed back into a boy.

DR: I don't remember that bit at the end 'cos isn't it near- at the end, he's got all that stuff in his house hidden away?

Peter: Yeah.

DR: Is it after that then?

Peter: Then the other witch that's survived, erm, who didn't get turned into a mouse ...er ...she went to his house and, then ...er

Claire: [whispered] Changed him back.

Peter: Changed him back.

DR: Ah! Yes, I do remember now. Gosh, I'd forgotten all about that.
Well I never! ... What's his name?

Claire: Erm, Luke. But it doesn't actually tell you in the book.

DR: Does it not?

Claire: In the movie [indecipherable]

DR: Who tells the story? I mean obviously Roald Dahl writes it but...

Claire: Er - Luke...the boy.

Peter: Er -

DR: He tells it himself - well maybe that's why he's not named.

Peter: It's like 'It all happened when we were', like, 'driving down - down this road to my grandmother's, and the car fell off

the rock. I was the only survivor' - things
like that, so it must be him who's telling it.

DR:       Right, so it's all told by him.

## 5. On the leader of the Secret Seven (Cloverdale, Group 2)

DR:       Is there- is there a leader of the Secret
          Seven? ...    [indecipherable]
          Is it one of the boys or girls?

Rebecca: It's a boy.

DR:       Mmm ...But you don't really mind?

Rebecca: No.

Emily:    No.

Matthew: As long as it's got dinosaurs
          in...[laughter]

Victoria: [lost in laughter] I think the leader of
          the Secret Seven's a girl.

DR:       You what, sorry?

Victoria: I think the leader's a girl.

DR:       You think it's a girl.

## 6. On the leader of the Secret Seven (Sprawldon, Group 10)

DR:       Who- Who's the leader of the- the group?

Deena:    Peter and Janet, I think ...is.

Sanjay:   Peter.

Zakir:    Peter.

DR:       Is it a boy or a girl?

Zakir:    I think it's a boy.

Sanjay:   Boy.

Danielle: Boy.

Deena:   Peter is.

### 7. Emma and William on 'Georgina' in the Famous Five  (Cloverdale, Group 4)

DR:        ...I want to know now your favourite character in a book, right?  The person in a book you like the best.

Emma:    I know.

DR:        What, Emma?

Emma:    I like Georgina, out of Famous Five.

DR:        Georgina. Right - why do you like her?

William:  [turning to Emma] George.

Emma:    Erm ...I don't know really.

### 8. Boy talking about having 'Matilda' as favourite character  (Sprawldon, Group 11)

DR:        Matilda, which some of you said you liked before - you particularly picked up on it Ahmed. Do you mind- I mean, the main character in that's a girl, isn't it?  Does that- Do you mind about that at all?  You don't mind reading books like that?

Irfan:     No.

DR:        Irfan says it doesn't matter at all - as long as it's a good book.

Irfan:     Because it is by a man.

Ahmed:   Yes.

James:    Yes.

Darren:   I'm not bothered who it's by or- what they've got in it.

9. Discussing whether **The Witches** is more
   of a boys' or a girls' book  (Cloverdale,
   Group 1)

DR:       Do you think **The Witches** is more of a
          boys' than a girls' book?
Claire:   I don't know, about-
Nicholas: Both the same.
David:    Probably both because it's about witches,
          which are women, but the star of it's a boy.
DR:       What do you say about that ... Claire?
Claire:   Cheek!
DR:       What do you think then? Do you disagree
          with Peter then, or what?
Claire:   Well ... there is horrible male people as
          well ...
DR:       What -
Claire:   ...like the Twits and things.
DR:       Like who?
Claire:   Like, there's Mr Twit, there's all the
          horrible giants ...as well as all the
          horrible witches ...[voice dropping to
          whisper] which are really women...
Peter:    And there's George's granny.
Claire:   I know.
Nicholas: Hmm [affirmative].
Peter:    Like you Claire.
Nicholas: [high pitched snigger].
Claire:   I'm only nine!
DR:       Do you think he gets more at women or
          men, or do you not think he makes any
          difference?
Peter:    Er... probably both, really.

DR: What do you think? Do you think 'both' as well?

Claire: Well ... giants aren't exactly men ... and witches aren't exactly ...[voice fades away completely]

DR: They - They aren't...?

Claire: Well they're dressed up.

DR: They're not actually women?

Claire: Mhm.

## 10. Why adults might not like **The Twits** (Cloverdale, Group 1)

DR: Do you think the book- I mean, I've heard some people say they don't like it - some adult people. Why do you think they might not like it?

Peter: Because its about two horrid grown ups. [laughter]

## 11. What happens at the end of **The Twits** (Sprawldon, Group 11)

Karl: ...because they do tricks and everything

DR: Yeah, but when they've done all that, when they've got rid of them. What happens to them then?

Karl: They get out, and try and torment the Twits.

DR: After they've got rid of the Twits and the Twits disappear.

Darren: Erm, they stay in the house.

Ahmed: They stay in the house.

## 12. What happens at the end of **The Twits** (Cloverdale, Group 1)

DR:      ...I'm thinking at the end. You know what the animals do at the end? ... What do they do?

Peter:   [indecipherable] so that nobody could look in and see them doing it.

Claire:  In the winter, they all go off to Africa.

DR:      Who do? Sorry.

Claire:  Muggle-Wump ... and his family...and they come back, and they rebuild the house in the monkey [indecipherable]

DR:      Sorry - is that in the story, you say?

Claire:  Yeah.

DR:      At the end of the story.

Claire:  Yeah, the monkeys are happy in the end.

DR:      So they don't go off to Africa, do they?

Claire:  Yeah [i.e. they do]

Nicholas: Yeah.

Peter:   Yeah. They wait in the treehouse until autumn, when the first leaves startin' , then ... then the Roly-Poly Bird takes them on a Roly-Poly airjet - or something like that.

## 13. Remembering Fred, followed by the Roly-Poly Bird's sex (Clogburn, Group 6)

DR:      Remember a character called Fred?

Simon:   Yeah, the postman.

DR:      The postman.

Lindsay: Yeah.

DR: Where does he come in?

Simon: At the end. When he's posting the letters and no one's in. He's knockin' on't door and no one answers, and, and all the clothes were on the floor ... at the end.

DR: Right. Er - the Roly-Poly Bird, going back to the Roly-Poly Bird is - I can't remember... Is it, is it a - is it a male bird or a female bird, do you know?

All: Female.

## 14. On sex of Roly-Poly Bird (Sprawldon, Group 10)

DR: How many are ... men characters in it, or male characters - and how many female, can you remember?

Deena: There's the three boys and Mr Twit, and...

Danielle: Monkeys.

Deena: Don't know - what's that exactly? [?]

Danielle: That's three, isn't it

DR: How-

Deena: That's three male and ......

DR: Yeah?

Deena: One female...no, two female, 'cos of the bird - I don't know about the monkeys.

DR: The bird's female, you think, and the monkeys?

Deena: Don't know about the monkeys.

DR: Sorry, the bird and ...what was it, Mrs Twit. Right, I see.

## 15. On Sex of Roly-Poly Bird (Cloverdale, Group 2)

DR:       ...Sorry, how many female - do you know what female means? I mean ladies, women, girls ... How many female characters are there in it?

Victoria: Mrs Twit.

DR:       Mrs Twit.

Victoria: Mrs Monkey.

Rebecca: Mrs Roly-Poly Bird.

DR:       Mrs Monkey - yeah, yeah. Right. Mrs Roly-Poly- Sorry, who did you say? Mrs-?

Rebecca: Roly-Poly Bird.

DR:       Roly-Poly Bird and Mrs...?

Emily:    Mrs Monkey.

DR:       Mrs Monkey. So there's three then. Yeah?

Emily:    Yeah.

## 16. On Beards (Clogburn, Group 6)

DR:       Yeah, what about him being hairy?

Stuart:   All his food goes in his beard.

Simon:    Yeah [laughing]

Lindsay:  [laughing] And in his beer.

Simon:    An' all his ... froth out of his beer always goes over it.

DR:       Yeah. What do you think of- You remember what it says about hairy- hairy men. Do you remember, from the beginning, the 'hairy ones' they call them? ... Do you remember, he talks about them at the beginning? Aaah! [unattributable]

DR: You can laugh out loud, you know ...Julie-it's quite alright. [suppressed giggle] You're going to burst if you don't let it out... What do you think? Do you know- do you know any hairy people then?

Simon: Erm.

Lindsay: [laughing] Yes, people's Dads.

Julie: Hee! hee! hee! [general glee]

DR: What do you think of hairy people with beards, or hairy people?

Stuart: I know one, but I'm not telling you.

DR: Why not?

Simon: I know what you said.

Stuart: He said- he said he said Mr Bamford. [explosive laughter]

DR: Who's that. Is that a teacher?

Stuart: He's a teacher.

Simon: He's the teacher next door to us. [more laughter]

DR: It's a good job I don't know your teachers, isn't it? So what do you think of hairy people, do you think ...

Simon: I don't like 'em.

DR: You don't like 'em.

Stuart: They're alright, but I don't like 'em when they've got hairs all over their face.

Lindsay: But sometimes it goes in their mouth [laughter].

DR: I mean what do you think when you grow older?

All: Ugh!

Simon: Shave it off!

Stuart: I'm not going to have a beard.

| DR: | You're not. |
|---|---|
| Stuart: | No, I'm not. |
| DR: | No? |
| Simon: | They're not [indicating girls, who giggle] |
| Stuart: | I should hope not, as well! [uncontrolled glee] |
| DR: | Have either of your Dads got beards? |
| Simon: | Yeah, my Dad's got a beard and a moustache. |
| DR: | Yeah - it's not like Mr Twit's, is it? |
| Simon: | No. [laughter] |
| DR: | No, no. Have either of your Dads got beards? |
| Stuart: | Sometimes, when he kisses me, right, it's always hurting [explosive laughter]. |
| Simon: | I know, it feels prickly. |
| Lindsay: | Like a thorn bush! |
| Stuart: | 'Cos, me Mum's, me Mum's boyfriend has a little one (DR: Mmm) but he's shaved it off now, and when he used to kiss you, it's all prickly. |
| Lindsay: | Like you fell in a thorn bush [said while laughing] |
| DR: | I see, right. Anyway, I think we'll, we'll go on to something else now. |

## 17. The 'Tom, Dick and Harry' theme (Cloverdale, Group 1)

| Claire: | You know the house and its got no windows? |
|---|---|
| DR: | Mmhm. |
| Claire: | Well they couldn't ...well they couldn't- well they couldn't- well they couldn't really survive with no fresh air, I think. |

DR:      Why do you think it's got no windows?

Peter:   'Cos Mr Twit said when they were building it that, who wants every Tom Dick and Harry looking in...

Claire:  [laughs]

Peter:   ...it didn't occur to him that windows might be for looking out of.

Claire:  [giggles]

DR:      What are you laughing at, Claire?

Claire:  Nothing.

DR:      Er- what do-...definitely laughing at something [laughter continues]. What are you laughing at Nicholas, but are trying not to laugh at?

## 18. Thinking through the story (Cloverdale, Group 3)

DR:      So you don't- you don't think it's true about beards, what he says generally?

George:  No.

Gemma:   No.

DR:      You don't, you think Mr Twit's like real, real people?

All:     No.

DR:      Do you think any of it's realistic, like real, could really happen... in The Twits?

All:     No.

DR:      No?

Gemma:   Er, yeah.

DR:      You do? What bits do you think, Gemma?

Gemma:   [laughs] Birds perching on the house.

DR:      Oh yeah, that's very true, yeah.

George:  That's true, but- and perching on the tree.

Gemma:   Yeah.

George:   But I don't think a Roly-Poly Bird
         would fly over here and be able to talk
         our language.

DR:       Is it like other books you know, or ...
         any other TV programme?

Gemma:   [Simult.] I don't think birds could talk,
         either.

George:   Bir-

Dan:      Parrots can.

Gemma:   Yeah, we- but I don't think-

George:   Yeah, but they don't understand the
         language.

Gemma:   I don't thi-

George:   They just copy.

Gemma:   I don't think they would have- they would
         have monkeys, even if they were monkey
         trainers.

Dan:      I can understand my cat's language,
         because, like when she's in the kitchen
         miaows I have to give her some food.

DR:       Mmm.

## 19.Violence in real life (Clogburn, Group 9)

DR:       Do you know many grown ups that behave
         like the Twits?

All:      Yeah.

DR:       You do!

Bushra:   Yeah.

Yusuf:    Yeah.

DR:       What sort of- what sort of things do they do?

Yusuf:    They hit you, the- sometimes they -

| Shital: | [Simult.] They hit you, they boss you around |
| DR: | Ah, they do that sort of thing. I see. The- |
| Yusuf: | [interrupting] I know someone, I know a man who killed this boy, right. This man called.... a boy, right, will you do a job for me... Then he did it. He said I'll give you a pound and, erm, and then after he... he went for some bread and he told him the address where to come to, and when he went there, erm, he called him in ... inside, then he killed him. |
| DR: | Oh. So you think they're like some adults in that way? |
| Yusuf: | Yeah. |
| Bushra: | Yeah. |
| DR: | But what about their playing, playing tricks. Just the things like where she puts her glass eye in his beer, and where, erm, the worms in the spaghetti - things like that. Are they like adults in that way? |
| All: | No. |
| DR: | What's that more like? |
| Shital: | Erm, horror films. |
| Yusuf: | Naughty things. |
| DR: | Is it, is it more like, is it more like grown up or what, or children...? |
| All: | Children. |
| DR: | 'Cos I think they're a bit like children in some way. Do you think that could be true? |
| Yusuf: | No. |
| Shital: | Yeah. |
| Bushra: | Yeah... They're like children. |
| Fatima: | Yeah. |
| DR: | But you- you don't Yusuf? |

Shital:    No, the way they hit children, they
           shouldn't hit childrens.
DR:        Mmhm. No. Right.
Yusuf:     No, I say no, I say no.
Shital:    You shouldn't hit childrens, when
           they're...
           [tape accidentally erased when
           playing-back for the group]

## 20. Language and Communication (Clogburn, Group 8)

Yusuf:     Yeah, because, you know my Mum, we-
           she doesn't- she doesn't bu- you know my
           Dad and Mum's teacher at coll- they're
           learning, so that my Dad has to talk English.
DR:        Sorry, but your Dad- your Mum doesn't
           speak...?
Yusuf:     English, so does my Dad not, but he
           knows some of it, but erm...
DR:        So does-
Yusuf:     When my Mum's teacher comes ...
DR:        Mmhm.
Yusuf:     Then my Dad has to and my Mum has to,
           er- my Dad and my Mum has to talk to me,
           to the teacher, English - because she's English.
DR:        Right. Right. So they have some problems
           that Muggle-Wump has, do they ...?
Yusuf:     Mm [nods].
DR:        ... speaking because they couldn't speak to
           the birds.
Bushra:    My grandad and my gran can't speak
           English.
Mandy:     The only- the only er 'hallo' I know...

| DR: | Do they have problems as well, or not? |
| Sandy: | [aside to Yusuf] You're getting all the speak [indistinguishable]... |
| DR: | What do you think about- do you think people all ought to speak the same language? |
| Yusuf: | No. |
| Sandy: | No. |
| DR: | No? You don't. |
| Sandy: | Yeah, I think everybody should speak ... English. |
| DR: | You think they should all speak English. What would you think about that, eh? |
| Yusuf: | No. |
| DR: | No? |
| Sandy: | Yeah. |
| Mandy: | I think they should speak their own language, the language that they, were... [indistinguishable - overtalked] |
| Sandy: | [now with back to Yusuf] I bet he wishes everyone speak er ... [turning to Yusuf] whatever you speak [laughter]. |
| Yusuf: | What did he say? |
| DR: | What do you think- do you think it's good having two languages? You've got an extra one, haven't you. |
| Yusuf: | Yeah, I can speak four- three... |
| Mandy: | [indistinguishable] |
| Yusuf: | I can speak three. No, I'm learning four now. I know Gujarati, English, er- Urdu, and I'm going to learn French in High School |
| DR: | Gosh - you gonna learn an awful lot of languages and you can speak to lots more people. |
| Yusuf: | And Germany. |

**Appendix V**
**A Selection of**
**Drawings and**
**Written Material**
**From Cloverdale**
**and Clogburn**
**Schools**

**A 1 - 4** Three drawings from Cloverdale (A1-3) and one from Clogburn (A4). Note that there are only three boys, rather than four, in A1 and A4. Also, note the window in the house - evident in the other pictures too. In A2 and A3 Mr Twit is firing the gun. Finally, note the dead tree has foliage in A3.

**B 1 - 3** Three drawings from Clogburn pupils, before they had heard more than half the story. In each of them, Mr Twit ends up shorn.

**C 1 - 4** Four pieces of written work from Clogburn pupils, done at the same time as the drawings. C1 and C2 were produced by B1 and B2 respectively. Note how each of them works towards some sort of resolution.

A1.

I liked the Twits very much. They make you laugh. My best part was when the boys got stuck on the tree.

Best books Roald Dahl

My favourite characters are in the book of Twits I liked them all best.

Monkeys

Glue (yuck)

Ahhh

Friday 19th April 1991

## Mrs Twit's Revenge

To pay Mr Twit back for the walking stick and the balloons Mrs Twit thought up a really horrid trick. When Mr Twit went asleep Mrs Twit went down stairs and got the chainsaw.

She pulled the cord and she cut up Mr Twit work.

Mrs Twit had to do it with a chainsaw because the scissors will break. Mrs Twit just finished cutting his hair off his head it took her an hour... Mr Twit got up he looked at his face and screamed that woke up Mrs Twit up. Mr Twit was shouting "Aaaaahhhh" for a very long time so we will have to stop. Goodbye.

C1.

Mrs Twits Revenge                Friday 19th April 1991

As soon as Mrs Twit came down her husband yelled while Mrs Twit grinned really Mr Twit was gobsmacked so he had a lay down while Mrs Twit had a good idea but wasn't ready to go into action she thought what Mr Twit would do to her but she couldn't think of any thing worse than cutting Mr Twits beard off because he was so fond of his beard Mrs Twit did not have a fit if anything but his stuff off but Mrs Twit wasn't bothered She went up stairs and finally the cut off and cried Mr Twit was restlaid so Mrs Twit decided to go and shear down stairs when Mr and Mrs Twit woke up Mr Twit yelled and Mrs Twit blushed loudly to Mr Twit was furiously when Mr Twit came down they had a terrible row so Mrs Twit packed her bags and left Mr Twit was so angry he shouted "Good riddance" And moctwit Fred happily ever after but we don't know about Mr Twit.

The End

C2.

b

Friday 19th April 1991

Mr Twits Revenge

Mr Twit diced to play a realy bad trick on mr Twit. She sad to her self - now now what trick shall I play on Ersy. When mr Twit went to bed mrs Twit marked down stairs. She went out got let of mud put the mud in the glass, and mixed it with water and sent out salt and pepper put dops of them in. wake up mr Twit" said mrs Twit. she gave him the hot chorlet he lived the hot chorlet he was sick. They never plaid tricks on each other a gain.

C4

---

Friday 10th April 1991

Mrs Twit's Revenge

To get Mr Twit back for the walking stick. She did something horred. Mr Twits worst fear was Soup. So Mrs Twit bought Some Soup. When Mr Twit came in to breakfast She told him to get a lunch. Mr Twit Shouted no you woman So when Mr Twit was drinking his beer She went to the table with a bowl of water and soap She took the beer and stated washing Mr Twit. then got the Srumps and washed his beah. and hair. He Shouted no no dont. When Mrs Twit was finished Mr Twit was very very clean.

C3

131

**Bibliography**

Anon (1980) 'Portrait of an anti-heroine', *Times Educational Supplement*, 5th December, p. 23.

Anon (1991) 'Children market grows, says BML', *The Bookseller*, 8th March, p. 677.

Applebee, A N (1978) *The Child's Concept of Story: Ages Two to Seventeen*, London: University of Chicago Press.

Aries, P (1973) *Centuries of childhood*, Harmondsworth: Penguin.

Atkinson, M (1984) *Our Masters' Voices: the Language and Body Language of Politics*, London: Methuen.

Baker, C D and Freebody, P (1989a) *Children's First School Books*. Oxford: Blackwell.

(1989b) 'Talk around text: constructions of textual and teacher authority in classroom discourse', in S. de Castell et al., *Language, Authority and Criticism: Readings on the School Textbook*, London: Falmer Press, pp. 263-83.

Bakhtin, M M (1981) *The Dialogic Imagination: four essays*. Austin: University of Texas Press.

Baldick, C (1983) *The Social Mission of English Criticism, 1848-1932*. Oxford: Oxford University Press.

Barthes, R (1975) *S/Z*. London: Cape.

Bartlett, F (1932) *Remembering: a Study of Experimental and Social Psychology*, Cambridge: Cambridge University Press.

Belsey, C (1980) *Critical Practice*. London: Methuen.

Bettelheim B (1976) *The Uses of Enchantment: the Meaning and Importance of Fairy Tales.* London: Thames & Hudson.

Bissett, D (1970) *Time and Again Stories.* London: Methuen.

Bourdieu, P (1984) *Distinction: a Social Critique of the Judgement of Taste*, Cambridge, MA: Harvard University Press.

Brompton, S (1986) 'Black looks at the littlest books', *The Times*, 24th November, p. 15.

Brown, G and Desforges, C (1979) *Piaget's Theory: a Psychological Critique*, London: Routledge & Kegan Paul.

Brown, G and Yule, G (1983) *Discourse Analysis*, Cambridge: Cambridge University Press.

Bruner, J (1986) *Actual Minds, Possible Worlds*, London: Harvard University Press.

Bruner, J (1990) *Acts of meaning*, London: Harvard University Press.

Bullock, A (1974) *A Language for Life, report of the Committee of Inquiry appointed by the Secretary of State for Education and Science under the chairmanship of Sir Alan Bullock*, London: HMSO.

Butler, D (1986) *Five to Eight*, London: Bodley Head.

Cameron, E (1972) 'McLuhan, youth and literature', *The Horn Book Magazine*, October, pp. 433-40.

(1978) 'A question of taste' *Children's Literature in Education*, No. 21, pp. 59-63.

Carpenter, H (1985) *Secret Gardens: a Study of the Golden Age of Children's Literature*, London: Allen & Unwin.

Carter, A (1990) *The Bloody Chamber and Other Stories*, Harmondsworth: Penguin.

Cass, J E (1977) *Literature and the Young Child*, Harlow: Longman.

Chambers, A (1985) 'The reader in the book', in A Chambers, *Booktalk*, London: Bodley Head, pp. 34-58.

Churchill, D (1981) 'Roald Dahl. The Twits' [a review] *School Librarian*, vol. 29 (3) p. 233.

Cicourel, A (1964) *Method and Measurement in Sociology*, New York: Free Press.

Coles, R (1986) *The Political Life of Children*. Boston: Houghton Mifflin.

Cott, J (1984) *Pipers at the Gates of Dawn: the Wisdom of Children's Literature*, New York: Viking.

Cox, B (1989) *English for ages 5 to 11*. (D.E.S. and Welsh Office). London: HMSO.

Coyle, M (ed) (1990) *Encyclopedia of Literature and Criticism*, London: Routledge.

Crago, M and Crago, H (1983) *Prelude to Literacy: a Preschool Child's Encounter with Picture and Story*, Carbondale: Southern Illinois University Press.

Creighton, S J and Owtram, P J (n.d.) *Child Victims of Physical Abuse: a Report on the Findings of NSPCC Special Units' Registry*. London: NSPCC.

Crowther, S (1986) 'Is it goodbye to 1984 and all that?' *English in Education*, vol. 20 (1), pp. 17-26.

Dahl, R (1964) *Charlie and the Chocolate Factory*, London: Cape.
(1968) *The Magic Finger*, London: Cape.
(1974) *Fantastic Mr Fox*, Harmondsworth: Penguin.
(1977) *Danny the Champion of the World*, Harmondsworth: Penguin.
(1978) *The Enormous Crocodile*. London: Cape.

Dahl, R (1981) *George's Marvellous Medicine*, London: Cape.
(1982) *The Twits*, Harmondsworth: Penguin.

(1983) *The Witches*, Harmondsworth: Penguin.
(1984) *Boy: Tales of Childhood*, Harmondsworth:
Penguin.
(1986) *The BFG*, Harmondsworth, Penguin.
(1987) *The Twits*, read by Roger Blake.
Audio-cassette. Temple Communications.
(1988) *Matilda*, London: Cape.

Daly, M (1987) *Webster's First New Intergalactic
Wickedary of the English Language*, Boston, Mass:
Beacon Press.

Davies, M M (1989) *Television is Good for your Kids*,
London: Hilary Shipman.

Dixon, B (1977) *Catching Them Young*, (2 vols)
London: Pluto Press.

Dodsworth, M (1991) 'The undermining of English:
how the National Curriculum threatens literature
teaching', *Times Literary Supplement*, 22nd February,
p. 11.

Doherty, B. (1987) 'Snowy story', *Times Educational
Supplement*, 13th February p. 48.
        (1989) *Tough Luck*, London: Collins.

Donaldson, M L (1986) *Children's explanations: a
Psycholinguistic Study*, Cambridge: Cambridge
University Press.

Douglas, M (1966) *Purity and Danger: an Analysis of
the Concepts of Pollution and Taboo*, London:
Routledge & Kegan Paul.

Doyle, B (1989) *English and Englishness.*
London: Routledge.

Duffy, M (1972) *The Erotic World of Faery,*
London: Hodder & Stoughton.

Eagleton, T (1983) *Literary Theory: an
Introduction.* Oxford: Basil Blackwell.

Edwards, D and Mercer, N (1987) *Common
Knowledge: the Development of Understanding in
the Classroom,* London: Methuen.

Fillingham, C (1989) Favourite books, favourite
authors: a consumer survey. *The Bookseller,* 10th
March.

Firestone, S (1979) 'Down with childhood', in M
Hoyles (ed) (1979) *Changing Childhood,* London:
Writers and Readers Publishing Cooperative.

Foucault, M (1979) *Discipline and punish,*
Harmondsworth: Penguin.
        (1980) *Power/Knowledge: selected
interviews and other writings, 1972-77,* Brighton:
Harvester Press.

Fox, C (1986) 'Poppies will make them grant', in
M Meek and C Mills (eds) *Language and Literacy
in the Primary School,* London: Falmer Press,
pp.53-68.

Fraser, E (1987) 'Teenage girls reading "Jackie"',
*Media, Culture and Society,* Vol. 9 (4), pp. 407-25.

Fry, D (1985) *Children Talk About Books: Seeing Themselves as Readers*, Milton Keynes: Open University Press.

Gilbert, P (1987) 'Post reader-response: the deconstructive critique', in B Corcoran and E Evans (eds) *Readers, Texts and Teachers*, Milton Keynes: Open University Press.

Gill, D (1989) 'National Curriculum ...acceptable authors?', *Multicultural Teaching*, vol. 7 (2), pp. 36-7.

Gilligan, C (1982) *In a Different Voice: Psychological Theory and Women's Development*, Harvard: Harvard University Press.

Gombrich, E (1977) *Art and Illusion: a Study in the Psychology of Pictorial Presentation*, London: Phaidon Press.

Goodman, K S and Goodman, G Y M (1977) 'Learning about psycholinguistic processes by analyzing oral reading', *Harvard Educational Review*, vol. 47 (3), pp. 317-33.

Goodnow, J (1977) *Children's Drawing*, London: Fontana.

Glastonbury, M (1980) Patriarchal attitudes: the classics, *New Statesman*, 14th November, p. 17.

Green, P (1959) *Kenneth Grahame, 1859-1932: a study of his life, work and times*, London: John Murray.

Haigh, G (1982) 'For non squiffletrotters only', *Times Educational Supplement,* 19th November, p. 35.

Hall, L (1983) 'A taste for greatness', *Times Educational Supplement,* 29th April, p. 55.

Heath, S B (1983) *Ways with Words: language, life, and work in communities and classrooms,* Cambridge: Cambridge University Press.

Hennegan, A (1988) 'On becoming a lesbian reader', in S Radstone (ed) *Sweet Dreams: Sexuality, gender and popular fiction,* London: Lawrence & Wishart, pp. 165-90.

Hill, G (1988) 'Bookworms: the inside story'. *The Times,* 29th March, p. 11.

Hodge, R and Tripp D (1986) *Children and Television: a semiotic approach,* London: Polity Press.

Hollindale, P. (1974) *Choosing Books for Children,* London: Elek.

Huck, C S and Young D A (1966) *Children's Literature in the Elementary School.* New York: Holt, Rinehart & Winston.

Hunt, P (1991) *Criticism, Theory and Children's Literature,* Oxford: Blackwell.

Hunter, I (1988) *Culture and government: the emergence of literary education*, London: Macmillan.

Ingham, J (1981) *Books and Reading Development: the Bradford Book Flood Experiment*. London: Heinemann Education.

Inglis, F (1981) *The Promise of happiness: value and meaning in children's fiction*. Cambridge: Cambridge U.P.

Iser, W (1974) *The Implied Reader: patterns of communication in prose fiction from Bunyan to Beckett*, London: John Hopkins University Press.
　　　　(1978) *The Act of Reading: a theory of aesthetic response*, London: Routledge & Kegan Paul.

Itzin, C (1985) 'Bewitching the boys', *Times Educational Supplement*, 27th December, p. 13.

Jackson, D (1983) 'Learning to become an active reader', *Use of English*, vol. 34 (2) pp. 59-67.

Jackson, R (1981) *Fantasy: the literature of subversion*, London: Methuen.

Jackson, S (1982) *Childhood and Sexuality*, Oxford: Basil Blackwell.

Jameson, F (1975) 'Magical narrative: romance as genre', *New Literary History*, No.7 pp. 135-63.

Kemp, G (1977) *The Turbulent Term of Tyke Tyler*, London: Faber & Faber.

Klein, G (1985) *Reading into Racism: bias in children's literature and learning materials*, London: Routledge & Kegan Paul.

Knight, R and Robinson, I (eds) (1988) *My Native English: criticism of an unnecessary crisis in English Studies*, Doncaster: Brynmill Press.

Landsberg, M (1988) *The world of children's books: a guide to choosing the best.* London: Simon & Schuster.

Lee, J (1984) 'For their own purposes - reading African and Caribbean literature with young black people', in J Miller (ed) *Eccentric Propositions: essays on literature and the curriculum*, London: Routledge & Kegan Paul, pp. 231-42.

Leeson, R (1985) *Reading and Righting: the past, present and future of fiction for the young.* London: Collins.

Lewis, C S (1969) 'On three ways of writing for children', in S Egoff et al. (eds) *Only Connect: readings on children's literature*, New York: Oxford University Press, pp. 207-20.

Lovell, T (1987) *Consuming Fictions*, London: Methuen.

Lurie, A (1990) *Don't tell the grown ups: subversive children's literature*, London: Bloomsbury Publications.

McDowell, M (1976) 'Fiction for children and adults: some essential differences', in G Fox et al. (eds) *Writers, Critics and Children*, London: Heinemann Education.

Macherey, P (1978) *A Theory of Literary Production.* London: Routledge & Kegan Paul.

Matthews, G (1980) *Philosophy and the Young Child*, London: Harvard University Press.
          (1984) *Dialogues with Children*, London: Harvard University Press.

Medway, P (1980) *Finding a Language: autonomy and learning in school.* London: Writers and Readers/Chameleon.

Mehan, H (1979) *Learning Lessons: Social Organization in the Classroom*, London: Harvard University Press.

Moss, G (1989) *Un/popular Fictions*, London: Virago Press.

Mulhern F (1979) *The Moment of Scrutiny*, London: New Left Books.

NATE (1985) *Alice in Genderland: reflections on language, power and control*, Sheffield: NATE.

Needle, J (1981) *The Wild Wood*, London: Andre Deutsch.

Nettell, S (1990) 'Short shrift for children's books', *The Author*, vol CI(1), pp. 12-14.

Newson, J and Newson, E (1970) *Four Years Old in an Urban Community*, Harmondsworth: Penguin.

Opie, I and Opie, P (1959) *The Lore and Language of Schoolchildren*, Oxford: Clarendon Press.

Peters, R S (1966) *The Concept of Education*, London: Routledge & Kegan Paul.

Peterson, C and McCabe A (1983) *Developmental Psycholinguistics: Three Ways of Looking at Children's Narrative*. New York: Plenum Press.

Piaget, J (1926) *The Language and Thought of the Child*, London: Routledge & Kegan Paul.
    (1951) *Play, dreams and imitation in childhood*. New York: W W Norton.

Pirani, F (1988) *Abigail at the beach*, London: Collins.

Postman, N (1982) *The Disappearance of Childhood*, New York: Delacorte.

Protherough, R (1983) *Developing Response to Fiction*, Milton Keynes: Open University Press.

Purves, A (1973) *Literature Education in Ten Countries: an empirical study*, London: John Wiley.

Ray, S (1982) *The Blyton Phenomenon: the controversy surrounding the world's most successful children's writer*, London: Andre Deutsch.

Rees, D (1988) 'Dahl's chickens: Roald Dahl', *Children's Literature in Education*, 19 (3), pp. 143-55.

Reid, J F (1977) 'Children's comprehension of syntactic features of extension readers', in J F Reid and H Donaldson, (eds) *Reading: problems and practices*, London: Ward Lock, pp. 382-91.

Reynolds, K (1990) *Girls Only? gender and popular children's fiction in Britain, 1880-1910*, London: Harvester Wheatsheaf.

Robertson, P (1976) 'Home as a nest: middle class childhood in nineteenth-century Europe', in L deMause (ed) *The History of Childhood*, London: Souvenir Press.

Rose, J (1984) *The Case of Peter Pan, or the Impossibility of Children's Fiction*, London: Macmillan.

Rose, N (1985) *The Psychological Complex: psychology, politics and society in England, 1869-1939*, London: Routledge & Kegan Paul.

Rustin, M and Rustin, M (1987) *Narratives of Love and Loss: studies in modern children's fiction*, London: Verso.

Sale, R (1978) *Fairy tales and after: from Snow White to E B White*, London: Harvard University Press.

Sandberg, R (1989) 'Who censors?' *Books for Keeps*, No. 58 p. 23.

Sarland, C (1982) 'Piaget, Blyton, and story: children's play and the reading process', *Children's Literature in Education*, vol. 16 (2), pp. 102-9.

Sarland, C (1983) 'The Secret Seven vs The Twits: cultural clash or cosy combination? *Signal*, No. 42, pp. 155-171.

Schlager, N (1978) 'Predicting children's choices in literature: a developmental approach', *Children's Literature in Education*, vol. 30 (4) pp. 136-42.

Shannon, P (1987) 'Unconscious censorship of social and political ideas in children's books', *Children's Literature Association Quarterly*, vol. 12 (2) pp. 103-5.

Shavit, Z (1986) *Poetics of Children's Literature.* Athens, GA: University of Georgia Press.

Shiach, D (1989) *Discourse on Popular Culture: class, gender and history in cultural analysis, 1730 to the present*, Cambridge: Polity Press.

Singer, J and Singer, D (1979) 'TV viewing, family style and aggressive behavior in pre-school children', quoted in M Green (ed) *Violence and the American family.*

Stanley, L (ed) (1990) *Feminist Praxis: research, theory and epistemology in feminist sociology.* London: Routledge & Kegan Paul.

Steedman, C (1982) *The Tidy House: little girls writing,* London: Virago Press.

Stones, R (1983) *'Book Choice: a bibliography of progressive books for young readers',* in R Leeson (1985) op. cit., pp. 195-247.

Stones, R and Mann, A (1979) *'Spare Rib' List of Non-Sexist Children's Books,* London: Spare Rib.

Stubbs, M (1983) *Discourse Analysis: the sociolinguistic analysis of natural language,* Oxford: Basil Blackwell.

Taylor, J L (1973) 'Voluntary reading habits of secondary school pupils', *Reading,* vol. 7 (3) pp. 11-18.

Townsend, J R (1976) *Written for Children: an outline of English-language children's literature,* Harmondsworth: Penguin.

Trelease, J (1984) *The Read-Aloud Handbook,* Harmondsworth: Penguin.

Tucker, N (1981) *The Child and the Book: a psychological and literary exploration.* Cambridge: Cambridge U.P.

Turner, V (1987) *From Ritual to Theatre: the human seriousness of play,* New York, PAJ Publications.

Volosinov, V (1973) *Marxism and the Philosophy of Language*, New York: Seminar Press.

Vygotsky, L (1962) *Thought and language*. Cambridge, MA: MIT Press.
(1978) *Mind in Society: the development of higher psychological processes*. London: Harvard University Press.

Walkerdine, V (1984) 'Developmental psychology and the child-centred pedagogy: the insertion of Piaget into early education', in J Henriques et al. (eds) *Changing the Subject: psychology, social regulation and subjectivity*, London: Methuen.
(1988) *The Mastery of Reason: cognitive development and the production of rationality*, London: Routledge.
(1990) *Schoolgirl Fictions*, London: Verso.

Wason, P C and Johnson-Laird, P N (eds) (1977) *Thinking: readings in cognitive science*, Cambridge: Cambridge University Press.

Wells, G (1986) *The meaning makers: children learning language and using language to learn*. London: Hodder & Stoughton.

Westall, R (1985) 'Why I read that book', in M Fearn (ed) *Only the Best is Good Enough: the Woodfield Lectures on Children's Literature, 1978-85*, London: Rossendale, pp. 16-31.

Whitehead, F (1966) *The Disappearing Dais: a study of the principles and practice of English teaching*, London: Chatto & Windus.

Whitehead F et al. (1977) *Children and their books*. Basingstoke: Macmillan/Schools Council.

Williams, R (1976) *Keywords: a vocabulary of culture and society*, London: Fontana.

Willis, P (1977) *Learning to Labour: how working class kids get working class jobs*. London: Saxon House.

Winn, M (1983) *Children without Childhood*, Harmondsworth: Penguin.

Wise, S and Stanley, L (1987) *Georgie Porgie: sexual harassment in everyday life*, London: Pandora Press.

Writers & Readers (1979) *Racism and Sexism in Children's Books*, London: Writers & Readers Publishing Cooperative.

Zipes, J (1979) *Breaking the Magic Spell: radical theories of folk and fairy tales*, London: Heinemann.
    (1983) *Fairy tales and the art of subversion: the classical genre for children and the process of civilization*, London: Heinemann.